Alexa's a SPY

AND OTHER THINGS TO BE TICKED OFF ABOUT

HUMOROUS ESSAYS ON THE HASSLES OF OUR TIME

Dorothy Rosby

Alexa's a Spy and Other Things to Be Ticked off About:
Humorous Essays on the Hassles of Our Time
Published by Unhinged Press
Rapid City, SD

ISBN: 978-0-578-60870-9

HUMOR / Essays

Cover and Interior design by Victoria Wolf

QUANTITY PURCHASES: Schools, companies,
professional groups, clubs, and other organizations may
qualify for special terms when ordering quantities of this
title. For information, email drosby@rushmore.com.

This book is printed in the United States of America

*For Wayne, who has heard me rant
on several occasions*

Contents

4. Where Are Your Manners?

5. What Is the Matter with Everyone?

6. Love Your Mother or She'll Kick Your...Behind

Introduction
Laugh, Die or Punch Someone

I never fell for that urban legend that was making the rounds a few years back—the one that said, on average, children laugh over three hundred times a day but adults laugh only seventeen. It just didn't add up. Unless they don't sleep, kids would have to laugh every few minutes all day long, and that wouldn't leave much time for throwing tantrums and bickering with their siblings.

I'm sure children do laugh more than adults though. Why wouldn't they? They aren't getting spam and robocalls all day long. They aren't paying a mortgage and worrying about their college fund. And most kids I know don't follow current events. I'd laugh too.

Speaking of current events, every time we turn on the news there's another disaster—an earthquake, a pandemic, an election. There's only one thing to do: Stop turning on the news. I'm joking. As citizens, it behooves us to stay informed. Plus, if we bury our heads in the sand, we leave our backsides vulnerable.

But with all we have to deal with, I think we'd be lucky to laugh seventeen times a day. It would be grand to laugh more, but counting how many times we do it might take some of the fun out of it. I've read that, among its many health benefits, laughter boosts immunity, lessens pain, lowers blood pressure and decreases stress hormones. It's not just that if you don't laugh you'll cry. If you don't laugh, you'll die.

Or punch someone. Then they might punch back. I think we can all agree laughing almost always beats both alternatives.

So what's stopping us from getting our recommended daily allowance of laugher? I'm going to tell you. What follows is a rant—a good-natured rant—but a rant nonetheless. It's about some of the things that keep us from laughing; the things we're irritated, angry or worried about; the things that sap our energy during the day and keep us awake at night.

Now that I think about it, that doesn't sound funny at all. Too late. I've already written the book. I hope you laugh at least seventeen times by the time you get to the end of it. But I don't offer a money-back guarantee.

Disclaimer: Portions of a few of these essays have appeared in some fashion in one of Dorothy's previous collections. She used them with her permission. She's nice like that.

CHAPTER ONE

Racking, Wracking and Cyberslacking

Racking, Wracking and Cyberslacking

I was racking my brain, trying to come up with a clever phrase to open this essay. As you can, see, I didn't. But that's because I got off track when I started to wonder if, instead of "racking" my brain, I might actually be "wracking" my brain. Either way, it was painful.

There was a day I would have consulted my trusty dictionary to answer such a question. But dictionaries are for people who don't need reading glasses—or need them and can find them. The rest of us can now go to the internet and consult a search engine. The print is larger and, for me, it's faster than finding my glasses.

After a quick search, I learned that I was most likely racking (stretching out, as with an ancient torture device) rather than wracking (ruining or destroying) my brain, which is lucky because I still need it.

I've been able to find answers to some of my most pressing questions on the internet, and some of them may even be right. For example, I found the cost of all the gifts listed in the "The Twelve Days of Christmas," though not why anyone would want ten lords a-leaping.

And I learned what's "corned" about "corned beef." In case you're wondering, the meat is cured by covering it with large kernels of salt that are called "corns of salt." And "corned beef" does sound better than "kerneled beef."

I was curious about what the majority of consumers call that bubbly beverage that comes in aluminum cans. And no, I don't mean beer—or champagne. As far as I know, champagne doesn't come in aluminum cans, but you could Google it to be sure. I typed in the phrase "soda or pop" and voila! Someone has thoughtfully created a map labeling each state: "pop," "soda," or "other," which seems like a funny name for a beverage.

Awhile back I was tempted to use a cliché I'd heard about lemmings following each other off a cliff to their deaths. But I know nothing about lemmings and was therefore not sure if they actually do follow each other off cliffs. Maybe I'd misunderstood; maybe it was not "lemmings," but "lemons" that follow each other to their deaths.

I turned to Bing the All Knowing and learned that the Norwegian lemming population level regularly rises to unsustainable levels, which causes it to crash. This abrupt drop has given rise to the myth of lemming mass suicide. I found no such information about lemons.

It's probably clear by now that I don't heed that old advice given to writers: "Write what you know." If I would have, I'd have run out of material a long time ago.

Why should writers stick to what we know when we've got Google, Webopedia, Bing, Baidu, Ask, Dogpile, Duck Duck Go, Yippy Search and more? (I personally don't use all of those. In fact, I'd never heard of some of them until I did a quick internet search for internet search engines.)

Back in the old days, if I wanted to know Barbie's full name (Barbara Millicent Roberts) or the birthstone for August (peridot), I had to check an encyclopedia—or just make it up. Now I go to Google the Omnipotent where, for all I know, someone else made it up.

And there are other dangers. One day while I was happily wandering around the World Wide Web searching for the difference between yams and sweet potatoes, I landed on a trap. Suddenly a bright red box popped up on my screen with the ominous message, "Your computer has been blocked. Your browser might have been hacked. Suspicious activity detected." Then there was a "ding, ding, ding" like I'd just breached security at a nuclear power plant.

In a panic, I called the number at the bottom of the screen and a very polite-sounding gentleman answered. I was just about to give him my credit card number when I experienced a rare bout of common sense. It occurred to me he may not be as nice as he sounded. I'm not either, so I told him, "Never mind. I don't think you can be trusted." Then I hung up, shut down my computer and came back later. All was well.

There's another danger of wandering around on the Web, and this one is more insidious. For me, searching for information on the internet is like following a butterfly. I land here, see something else that catches my fancy, follow that, land there and so on and so forth until the afternoon is gone and I can't remember why I started searching.

I once wrote an essay about the foods served at Super Bowl parties. That's always been more important to me than the game, no matter who's playing. But when I searched for "Super Bowl food," I discovered there were more than three million results. Do you know how long it takes to read three million results? Neither do I. But I almost missed the Super Bowl party trying to find out.

And a few months back, I went to the Web wondering if I could freeze butter. I'd picked some up at the grocery store, brought it home and discovered I already had a pound in my refrigerator. Fortunately you *can* freeze butter and, as it turns out, raw egg whites and tomato sauce. But don't freeze cooked egg whites, cheese or macaroni, at least not if you want to eat them someday. I know that because I followed a link and then another one and another one. Meanwhile my extra butter was melting on my kitchen counter.

I recently went online to find out how many tiles there are in a Scrabble game. In case you were wondering, there are ninety-eight letter tiles and two blank ones. We have a scrabble game, but I haven't seen it in years, so I decided it would be faster to search online than it would be to locate my own game. And it was faster, even when you take into account that I got sidetracked following a link to a story on seventeen ways to cheat at Scrabble.

Researching trivia has replaced walking back and forth to the refrigerator as my favorite way to avoid doing actual work at my computer. As I write, questions pop into my head and most of them have nothing to do with what I'm working on. For example, how many licks does it take to get to the center of a Tootsie Pop? Knowing that it's approximately 252 is useful when Tootsie Pops play a role in what I'm writing, but up until this moment they never have.

Worse, I've wasted time researching when I could have been working or even licking an actual Tootsie Pop myself.

If you're thinking it couldn't have taken that long, you've apparently never blown an afternoon following one link and another and another until you've completely forgotten what your original question was.

Let me demonstrate. Let's say I want to make a better meatloaf. Before I type the word "meatloaf" into the search bar, I have to get past my newsfeed. I seldom do.

There's a story about what I should never do to an avocado (bake it), why they have shoulder buttons on women's coats (to hold your purse in place), and how to pronounce Princess Eugenie's name. I've never given this a thought, but now that you mention it…I click on the link and see a photo of Princess Eugenie wearing what looks like a satellite dish on her head. I love hats; I'm less fond of satellite dishes.

Suddenly, I'm overcome with curiosity. Why do royals wear such goofy hats? I type the question into the search bar and an explanation appears, but I don't read it because my attention is caught by a sidebar: "The best haircuts for older women." Now there's news I can use. I start scrolling. I'm at thirty-two—the haircut, not the age—when my attention is snagged by another sidebar, "Why you shouldn't add milk to scrambled eggs." I don't, but I can't help wondering why I shouldn't. It's a free country after all. I click on the link and up pops a story and photo of scrambled eggs. Dang, I'm hungry. What should I make for dinner?

I have just whiled away an hour, and I still don't know how to pronounce Eugenie, why she wears those bizarre hats, what my next haircut should be or how to make a better meatloaf. So if you want to know how, I'd suggest you don't look it up.

There's a silver lining though. When children of long ago had questions, their mothers often sent them to the encyclopedia. "Look it up," they said, and obedient children did as they were told. More clever children realized their mothers didn't know the answer but were too embarrassed to admit it, so they gave up and ran off to play. And foolish children asked older siblings who purposely misled them. That explains why, to this day, many adults think camels store water in their humps and chocolate milk comes from brown cows.

Things have changed. Today's children look up information without being told to. And why not? Asking Siri or searching the internet is so easy even an adult can do it. And we do—all day long.

Alexa, Siri and Cortana
Walk into a Bar

Ann says her husband is having an affair. She told a group of us having lunch that she'd seen them together. "You know her," Ann said. "She's three feet wide and has one big eye in the middle of her forehead. Her name is Magna…Magna Vox."

We all laughed—sort of. Turns out several of my friends suspect their husbands of having Magnas or Sonys on the side.

Lilly said that when she and James were newly-weds, the first thing he did when he came home from work was kiss her. Now, five years later, the first thing he does is turn on the television. "One night, I asked him if the TV could wait since we hadn't seen each other all day, but he said he hadn't seen his television all day either."

"Oh, to have Jeff pay attention to me like he pays attention to that television," agreed Ann.

"Be careful what you wish for," said Sandy. "I read that the average adult watches almost five hours of television a day. Would you really want a man staring at you, a blank look on his face, for five hours every day?"

But Ann said Jeff at least smiles at the television. "Sometimes he even talks to it, and once he actually said 'I love ya, man,' to a TV sportscaster."

Sandy said Neil uses the television as an escape.

"What's he escaping from?" we asked.

"Near as I can tell, the supper dishes."

"At least he's watching it," said Karen. She said her husband wanders in, turns on the television, then wanders back out, leaving their bulldog Brutus to watch TV alone. "I bet he's spent five years of his life watching television—and those are dog years."

We all agreed it can't be healthy for man or beast to watch that much TV. Ann said Jeff's idea of exercise is wandering around the living room looking for the remote control.

But Lilly warned us about turning off the television completely. "We tried that during Screen-Free Week last spring. I knew we needed the TV back when James asked me how long my hair has been gray."

I told my friends there's another woman in my husband's life too, but she's not a TV. "We met her a few years ago while we were traveling and we both liked her right away, but my husband really fell for her. Her name is Garmin Nuvi."

"She sounds exotic," said Ann.

"She is. She's also smart and attractive and unlike me, good with directions. I can't compete with that."

Garmin is a GPS device and I told my friends I'm not surprised my husband is attracted to her. "I wouldn't call her a cheap date, but she is low maintenance. She doesn't fiddle with the radio or complain about the air conditioning. She never has to stop to use the restroom. And she doesn't sleep across entire states—unless we want her to."

"I bet she doesn't get grumpy when she doesn't eat either," said Karen who has traveled with me.

Sandra said her husband is also fond of Garmin.

"She has a lovely voice but she sounds vaguely familiar. I wonder if she used to have a different job. I could swear she put me on hold once."

"Yeah, she sounds nice enough," I agreed. "But she's bossier than I am. Turn here, turn there, do this, do that. I could never get away with that."

"Maybe your husband tolerates it from her because she knows what she's talking about," said Karen. "And I bet she never says, 'Slow down' or 'Are we there yet?'"

I gave her my whose-side-are-you-on look. But I had to admit that "recalculating" is probably less annoying than "I told you so."

"She is really smart," said Sandra. "She can speak more than fifty languages in all sorts of voices and accents. Plus she can do math calculations, convert Celsius to Fahrenheit instantly and tell us the time in Tokyo."

"La-de-da," I said. "It's not like I'll ever be driving in Tokyo. And she isn't perfect by a long shot. She mispronounces names, and more than once she's taken us to businesses that aren't there anymore. Sure, at her best, Garmin is a calm reassuring voice in the midst of confusion. But at her worst, she's just a backseat driver without the cuss words."

"I don't know," said Sandra. "She's winning me over. I appreciate the way she gives directions without, you know, directions. East, west, north, south never work for me."

I had to admit, I appreciate that Miss Nuvi says "turn right" and "turn left" too. Even I can handle that, thanks to the hint I've used ever since I was a child: I write with my right. "And she never uses my least favorite phrase in the world of navigation: 'You can't miss it!' Is it blocking the road? On fire? No? Then I can miss it."

"She's friendly and helpful and she beats folding a map," said Sandy.

"And don't be so hard on your husband. We all know who your real BFF is," said Ann.

"Me? Who?"

"You're pretty tight with Miss Siri iPhone. You do have a tendency to anthropomorphize."

"And you have a tendency to use big words." I punched my phone and asked, "What does 'anthropomorphize' mean?"

Siri said, "'Anthropomorphism' means the attribution of human characteristics or behavior to a god, animal or object."

I couldn't deny it. I've named every car I've ever

owned. I talk to inanimate objects when they don't work right. (Maybe "talk" isn't the right word.) And I once bought the smallest Christmas tree on the lot because I felt sorry for it. My husband said, "It doesn't care. It's dead." But I cared.

"I suppose it's possible I'm seeing some human characteristics in my iPhone. But that's only because she has them." I pressed the button, and asked, "Siri, are you human?"

"Close enough."

"See. She's not perfect though. She interrupts me mid-text to correct my spelling. She's worthless if I forget to charge her. And her directions aren't always accurate, which is one thing she and I have in common. But her flaws only make her seem more human."

"No, she's smarter than a human—at least she's smarter than this human," said Lilly, gazing lovingly at her iPhone. "If I ask her what 590 times 750 is, she can tell me faster than I can find her calculator to figure it out myself."

"Yes," I agreed. "And she admits it when she doesn't know something. I wish more humans did that."

"She never loses her temper. Not many humans

remain calm when you push their buttons," said Lilly. "Or drop them on their head. Or repeatedly ask them if they're human."

"She's not just a companion," I said. "She's like a devoted employee. My friend Wikipedia calls Siri a 'personal assistant and knowledge navigator.' I think that suits her. She does everything except clean my house—as long as I pay my cell phone bill."

"So Siri, Cortana and Alexa walk into a bar," said Lilly.

"And…"

"They fire the bartender and start taking orders. But it's no joke. It could happen. I think they're in cahoots."

"Don't get me started on Alexa," said Ann. "Oh, too late. Today when Jeff was cuddled up on the couch watching Magna, he asked Alexa to dim the lights and get them a beer."

"Did she?"

"I don't know. He was still waiting when I left."

"My kids keep asking Alexa to clean their room," said Sandy. "And she spoils them. If I hadn't intervened last night, she'd have ordered them two extra-large pizzas, breadsticks and a side of chicken wings."

"I wouldn't trust her around your children,"

said Lilly. "Haven't you seen those creepy commercials? She's a fake person worming her way into your family. I think she's a spy."

"I think so too," I said. "And I heard she's dating HAL."

Hapless and App-less

I recently had an experience that left no doubt in my mind that the world has changed, and me with it. And yes, I realize the world changed a long time ago. But I took a little more time.

Here's what happened: I saw a magazine advertisement touting a restaurant's carryout menu. The headline read, "Start your meal with one of these sharable apps." And I thought, "Cool. If I lived near that restaurant, I could order carryout with a smartphone application." Or at least I could if I was as smart as my smartphone. I probably am not, considering it took me an embarrassing amount of time to realize they didn't mean apps, as in "applications," they meant apps, as in "appetizers."

How strange that I, who only updates my technological devices when the old ones stop working, would jump to the technology conclusion so fast. I've been eating regular meals for more than half a century, many of them at restaurants. That's considerably longer than I've had a smartphone. Plus, given the choice between appetizers and applications, I would choose appetizers anytime.

But there's an app for everything, including ordering food. An application (or "app") is, of course, software that you can download onto your computer or cellphone to help you perform important tasks or waste monumental amounts of time, whichever the case may be.

With the right apps, you can use your phone to track your budget or play a rousing game of "Plants Versus Zombies." You can plan your grocery list with your phone or pretend to shave with it. You can watch movies or navigate with map apps. You can; I can't. How could I read a map on an itty-bitty screen when I can't even read the old-fashioned variety on a giant sheet of paper? The only advantage I see to a map app is that I don't have to fold it.

iPhone's iDrag Paper app allows the user to unroll a roll of toilet paper on your screen. Both cats and small children enjoy this activity in real life, but I don't think many of them have iPhones. A friend of mine tried to convince her young granddaughter that unrolling a picture of toilet paper on her phone would be just as fun as unrolling the real deal. The child was unconvinced and I don't think my cat would fall for it either.

The Weight Loss Coach app assigns simple daily tasks to help you create a healthier lifestyle, then tracks how well you're doing right up until the moment you get annoyed with it and toss your phone into the dumpster behind the donut shop.

The myVertical app measures how high you jump, which is useful information if you're a high jumper or a basketball player. For more height, you could just throw it in the air rather than putting it in your pocket like you're supposed to, but that would be cheating. Also stupid. And unless you're a really good catcher, it could render all your other apps useless.

And you don't want to do that. Apps have taken

over our lives though it may be more accurate to say the smartphones you load them on have taken over our lives.

If you had told me twenty years ago that some-day, I would replace my telephone because it stopped texting, I would have said, "It stopped what?"

But that's what I did not long ago. And I'd do the same if it stopped receiving email, or keeping my calendar, or letting me play "Doodle Jump." I'm joking. I've never downloaded "Doodle Jump." But I do think I've reached a point where I use my phone for non-phone tasks more than I use it for its origi-nal purpose. You remember: making and receiving phone calls. That's because my new phone can do practically everything except the laundry—and I might find out she does that too once I get to know her better.

You're probably wondering how I know my new phone is a she. I'll tell you how: because she talks and she has a lovely female voice. And I don't just mean, "Please hang up and dial again." The other day she said, "I think therefore I am, but let's not put Descartes before the horse." I'm not making that up. She's a show-off.

Maybe it's time to do away with the word

"telephone" altogether and call our phones what they really are: smart personal assistants who, among their many talents, can also make and receive phone calls. I suppose that's not as catchy as smartphone and it takes up a lot of space in an advertisement.

It's not even 6 a.m. as I write this, and I've already used my smart personal assistant five times, and not once to make a call—lucky for you if you're on my contact list.

I checked the time, sent a tweet, read my email and asked her to check the weather for me. When I thanked her she said, "Your satisfaction is all the thanks I need." I think she's still trying to impress me.

Then she reminded me about a relative's birthday, so I asked her for the address so I could send a card. I'm still waiting for her to fill it out and mail it for me.

If I wanted, I could spend the day with my smart personal assistant, listening to music, hanging out on Facebook, or even watching movies with her, though I'm not sure why I would do that since I have a television screen the size of Seattle in my basement.

Nor do I necessarily want to read an entire novel on a device no bigger than a deck of cards, but I could. Or maybe she'd read to me. She does math problems if I ask her to. I wish I'd had her when I was in school.

If I get lost, which I often do, I can ask my smart personal assistant for directions. And if the electricity goes out, I can use her flashlight app. She's easier to find than my old-fashioned flashlights because she rings sometimes.

No, she's not perfect. She tries to correct my spelling and she's not as smart as she thinks she is. When I texted my son that we were going "canoeing," she guessed I meant "canning." Clearly she doesn't know me very well yet. And she occasionally gets her directions wrong, which is the only thing we have in common.

Plus there are a lot of things she can't do. She can't balance my checkbook. She can't warn me not to back out of the garage while I'm texting. She can't dust my living room.

But she does a lot. And all she asks of me is that I keep her battery charged. That and pay our cellphone bill on time.

One wonders what will become of the manufacturers of cameras, alarm clocks, calculators and all sorts of other devices now that so many people have smart personal assistants who, among their many talents, can also make and receive phone calls. And what will become of us when we lose our smartphones?

Imagine with me…

You see a woman digging through her purse like a starving dog digging for a bone. I'll bet my iPhone she's in the throes of that particular kind of anxiety attack one has when one realizes one's smartphone with all its fancy apps and functions has gone missing. I'm very responsible with my phone, so I've never experienced it myself. But I know the symptoms when I see them.

If you listen closely, you may hear some colorful language, even from victims with no previous history of it—not that this particular victim has no previous history of it. You may hear her muttering, "I downloaded Maps, the Weather Channel and the Merlin Bird ID app. Why didn't I download the Find My Phone app?"

Keep watching, and you'll see her search her pockets, shopping bags, briefcase or whatever else she's carrying. Then she'll expand her search to the pockets, shopping bags and briefcases of anyone standing nearby—with or without their permission.

If the cellphone still isn't located, and it probably won't be, our hapless—and now app-less—victim will begin to order those around her to call my number. Did I say *"my* number?" I meant *her* number. Call *her* number and she'll rush around, head cocked this way then that, listening carefully, and muttering that she'll never silence her phone again no matter how annoying it will be to everyone else when it goes off in church the next time.

She's panicking now, not only about the cost of replacing her phone, but about how much she's going to miss it now that it's gone. As we've already established, her very smart smartphone is not just her phone; it's her smart personal assistant who, among its many talents, can also make and receive phone calls. The thing has more uses than baking soda and duct tape combined. As much as she uses it, it's a wonder she ever puts it down long enough to misplace it.

And yet, she does—often. And she did—again, unless she dropped it, in which case, it's probably been run over in the parking lot by now.

Or maybe someone picked it up first. And maybe that someone is honest, and will make every attempt to return it. Or maybe that someone will not.

If she has any imagination at all—and it should be clear by now that she does—she thinks about how the thief will somehow manage to figure out her password. Then, with all the information that's stored on her phone, he'll take over her life and be more successful at it.

She decides she must retrace her steps. She reaches for her car keys and...what's that? It's her smart personal assistant who, among its many talents, can also make and receive phone calls. It's right where it's been all along, in the bottom of my purse. I mean *her* purse. It's right there in the bottom of *her* purse.

Passwords
and Pinheads

Four times I typed in my password and four times a message popped up on my computer screen telling me I was mistaken. How could that be? I've been to that particular website hundreds of times, but now it was being obstinate. So was I.

Each time I typed my password, I typed it more slowly and with a little more force. If the website hadn't had a four-strikes-and-you're-out policy, I'd have busted my keyboard. But after the last failed attempt a message popped up telling me to contact the site administrator. That's when it came to me. I had definitely been typing the right password—for the wrong website.

That was almost as aggravating as forgetting my PIN one day when I went to get money from the automatic teller machine. Maybe I was feeling pressured because there was an unusually long line behind me. Or maybe I was excited because normally if I'm in an unusually long line, I'm at the end of it.

Whatever the case, I panicked. As you can imagine, that did nothing to help me remember my PIN. It didn't come back to me until I'd driven around to the back of the long line, where I'm more accustomed to being.

I had to activate a new credit card recently and the customer service representative asked me to make up a four-digit code that would be hard for anyone else to guess but easy for me to remember. I told her that, number one, I am sick to death of codes, passwords and PINS. And number two, nothing is easy for me to remember.

The customer service representative said that a password was not absolutely necessary—unless I want quick efficient service in the future. Much to her surprise, I chose to go without quick efficient service.

The poor woman couldn't have known that when I called my internet provider for help recently, they wanted my password. This was understandable and fine with me, except that I didn't know I had one.

Nor could she have known that I had just spent a month in email negotiations with the company that sold me my virus protection software. They warned me that my service would soon expire and they needed my password in order to sell me more. Again, I had no recollection of ever having had a password and was, therefore, hard pressed to remember it.

Incidentally, they also wanted my computer's nickname. While I have been known to call my computer an assortment of nicknames, I would be embarrassed to share most of them.

It's not that I have a poor memory. I remember a lot of things. I remember my husband's birthday, my son's birthday and my birthday. I remember my husband's cellphone number, my cellphone number and the password to unlock my cellphone. I remember both of my email addresses, my mailing address and my former employer's mailing address. I remember the PIN for my bank account, my social security number and my sister's social security number. I have no idea why, but I do. Maybe it will come in handy when I retire.

My head is full of numbers, codes and passwords. I am crunched by numbers, numbed by numbers. It's no wonder I'm off by two years every time I write the year and by ten or fifteen pounds every time I give my weight.

Really how can I be expected to remember any more PINs, passwords or computer nicknames unless I write them down or use the same one for everything, which is apparently a bad idea? That would make my life so much easier—until some contemptible scoundrel figured it out and assumed my identity. And then my life wouldn't be easy at all, though it would be fine for the scoundrel.

And it's people like that—identity thieves, cyber scum and the like—who are to blame for the innumerable PINs, passwords and usernames that are spreading like a cancer across this land. If it weren't for them, we could get by with our names and an occasional "please" and "thank you." Curses on them all! May they suddenly need passwords to use their own bathrooms.

Until they get real jobs or we can use retinal scans and thumbprints to access everything from iTunes to our bank accounts, we will continue to need PINS, passwords and usernames. So as a public service, I'm offering a few helpful tips for coming up with secret codes. You can thank me by sending me your PIN.

1. Create an acronym, for example, HSHttYO (Hackers should have their toenails yanked out) or HWhoIT (Here's wishing hives on identity thieves).

2. Try mixing CaPital and LOwerCase LeTTers. Just make sure you remember which letters you made cApITAL and which ones you made loWERcASE.

3. Use phonetic replacements like LUV2LAF or hate2getrippedoff.

4. Deliberately misspell a word in your password to make it harder to crack. It also makes it harder to remember, but that's beside the point. Try something like EggselentPASSWEIRD or PLEESdon'tSTEELfromME.

5. Pick something that's easy for you to remember, but hard for a cyber scoundrel to guess. That means your birthday isn't a good choice, even though presumably you can remember it on most days. Try your first car's nickname or your height and weight combined. No, maybe not your weight.

That could change.

6. Tempting as it is, don't use the same password for everything. Life would be grand if we could use a password like "allpeople-R-honest" and "Itrustevery-1" for all of our accounts, but that isn't recommended, either as a password or as a way of life.

7. Finally, never give your password or PIN to anyone else—except me. I'm joking. Don't give it to me either. I don't want any more.

While
We Wait

I am not staring. That would be rude. I'm observing. I'm sitting in the waiting room at my dentist's office along with four other people. One is talking on his phone and the other three are contemplating their phone screens. Trust me; they wouldn't notice if I was staring anyway—which I'm not.

I'm not judging either. It's all I can do to keep from pulling out my own smartphone, checking my email, sending a text or two and telling all my Facebook friends where I am. I'm sure they'd be interested to know I'm having my teeth cleaned today.

But I refrain. I believe there are benefits to waiting without an electronic pacifier. Chief among them is learning to wait, which has never been one of my strong suits.

It's not my fault. I've had bad experiences waiting. Once at a restaurant my husband and I waited to be seated for what seemed like hours but was probably only forty-five minutes. It's a good thing we finally checked to see where our names were on the list, because they weren't on the list.

Worse than that, I once spent what seemed like days, but was probably only thirty minutes, waiting in an examination room. Finally I stuck my head into the hallway and asked a nurse if my doctor had been called away on an emergency. She was as shocked to see me as she would have been to see the doctor. He was out of town that day.

It's experiences like those that keep me from taking this patience thing too far. If I were better at waiting I might still be sitting there. Yes, I could stand to improve at the waiting game, though "game" makes it sound a lot more fun than it is.

I've developed a routine for those times when

I'm forced to wait, whether it's in a restaurant, at the mechanic shop or in line at a public restroom.

Instead of taking out my phone first thing I force myself to relax and observe my surroundings. Anyone watching me would think I was casing the joint, but nobody is watching me. They're all looking at their phones.

I check out the décor or lack of it. What's the layout? Where's the drinking fountain? Do they have coffee? I don't drink coffee, but if they have coffee maybe they have tea—or cocoa or a sundae bar. (Obviously I've never seen a sundae bar while I've been waiting in line at a public restroom—nor would I want to.)

Where are the exits? Where's the thermostat? I never touch it, but it's not like the people staring at their phones would notice if I did.

If the waiting room has a television, I look for the remote. I don't ever change it, or at least I don't ever admit to changing it. But who would see me if I did? They're too busy looking at the itty-bitty screens in their hands to notice what happens to the big one in the corner.

Finally I observe my fellow waiters—as in "those who wait," not "those who serve those who wait."

But what a good idea.

What does everyone look like? What are they wearing? If they're talking on their phones, what are they talking about? I'm not snoopy; I'm interested.

After I've run out of things to look at, I start the relaxation portion of my routine. Feel free to try it. And don't worry; you don't have to get down on the floor and do a pretzel pose. Hopefully you won't be relaxing long before it's your turn with the doctor, the table in the restaurant or the public restroom stall. If you're like me, it would take you more time just to get yourself situated that way—and probably longer to get back up. And you don't want to be down on the floor in a public restroom anyway.

Let me demonstrate: I take a deep breath, but not too deep if I'm waiting in a public restroom. Then I focus on my breath. Breathe and breathe. Good gravy! These pants are cutting me in half. I squirm and tug and in the process, my sweater gets wadded up. I adjust it, then I push the hair out of my eyes, clear my throat and scratch my chin. Dang it! There's a whisker growing there again. I'll get that when I get home.

Breathe, breathe. I relax each part of my body starting at the top of my head and working my way down. I've just reached my forehead when my cellphone rings. I ignore it. I breathe. It rings again. Oh heck. I've been listening to everyone else talk on their phones; they shouldn't mind if I talk on mine.

The caller informs me that her company is detecting a large amount of junk on my computer. Thanks to the patience I've gained from spending half my life waiting, I'm able to tell her that I'm also detecting a large amount of junk—on my telephone. And why doesn't she get a real job? But I mean that in the nicest possible way.

Maybe I spoke louder than I thought I did because everyone is looking at me now. I ignore them and breathe, breathe, relaxing my face, my neck, my right shoulder, my belly. My belly? That's not right. I wonder if I'll get out of here by lunchtime. Right arm, right hand, peanut butter. Peanut butter cups sound really good right now. Left shoulder, left arm. What? Wait a minute! It should be my turn. I was here before they were!

Left leg? Right leg? Whatever. I relax until I can't stand it anymore. Then and only then do I take out my phone. As you can see, in this way I'm becoming more patient, theoretically anyway. And the bonus—and this is no small thing: I'm also reducing my chances of leaving my phone all over town.

Personal Assistant
or Peeping Tom

I knew it. I'm being watched. I've thought so for a long time and now I know it for sure. How? My husband and I have been traveling. We're just preparing to leave our hotel when I notice a message on my cell phone saying that local transit system information has been added to the maps on my phone. We have a car; we won't be needing the transit system, but still, how thoughtful. And how weird.

Who added the information to my phone maps and how did they know I was here? Half the time, *I* don't know where I am. I can't decide if it's reassuring or creepy that someone else does.

And it's not just my smartphone watching my every move. Amazon knows what I want before I want it. They send me half a dozen emails every day telling me I'd probably like this or that, and sometimes they're right. I probably would. I see a day coming when they deliver products we haven't even ordered yet because they're so sure we will.

My Fitbit knows when I am sleeping. It knows when I'm awake. It knows how many steps I take, so I better walk more, for goodness sake. It's like Santa Clause without the gifts.

The all-knowing, all-seeing Facebook regularly names people it thinks I might know. And I do know many of them. It suggests people I should send birthday greetings to, and it's right; I probably should. It puts ads on my page promoting products and events it thinks I'll be interested in, and sometimes I am.

Pandora knows my taste in music. Twitter knows my taste in timewasting drivel. Google knows my questions before I ask them. And LinkedIn knows what jobs I should apply for if the one I have now falls through because I'm spending too much time on social media.

I can't decide if I'm being followed by a team of very efficient personal assistants or a gang of peeping toms. Sometimes I'm annoyed that they watch my every move. Other times I think they're taking over my life and doing a better job with it. Sometimes I think they interfere; other times I wish they'd do more. Why can't they message me that we're out of milk before I get all the way home and have to go back to the store? Why can't they load and unload the dishwasher?

Mostly my stalkers help me navigate through my life metaphorically and geographically. And I hate to admit it, but I'm starting to wonder how I would get along without them. They must wonder too. Before I started working from home there was a message on my cellphone every morning telling me what route I should take to work. How did it know? I didn't remember adding my location to my phone and probably couldn't if I tried. And why would I? I already knew how to get there.

Once I was at work, my phone told me the best route back home. I don't know what's more disturbing: that it knows where I live, or that it doesn't think *I* do.

No Child Left
(on Their) Behind

I haven't told my husband this yet, but I've made
a unilateral decision. This spring, we're going
to observe Screen-Free Week. I don't normally
approve of unilateral decisions in marriages, but
I'm supporting this one because I'm the one who
made it.

Screen-Free Week is an annual, international
celebration when we swap digital entertainment
for real life. I call it No Child Left on Their Behind
Week. No adult either.

According to ReportLinker, the average American household has 7.3 screens—tablets, PCs, notebooks, smartphones and televisions. We're a nation with more screens than people. And screens do have some advantages over people, mainly remote controls and off buttons. The problem is, we don't use the off buttons very much. A lot can happen in our homes, our communities and our country while we sit on the sofa playing "Candy Crush," too chubby to get up and defend ourselves.

According to the Campaign for a Commercial-Free Childhood, children eight and younger average two and a quarter hours of screen entertainment every day. Tweens spend an average of almost six hours in front of a screen, and teens average nearly nine hours, not counting what they use for school work. Maybe it's not as bad as it sounds. Maybe that includes the time they spend helping adults with our screens.

And before you judge them, you should know that adults spend more than eight and a half hours a day staring at screens, according to the market-research group Nielsen. And four hours and forty-six minutes of that is spent watching television and complaining that there's nothing on.

When you watch too much television, you see things no one should ever see. And I'm not just talking about violence and vulgarity, though there's plenty of that. I'm talking about…well…dumb stuff.

I once watched a man on television attempt to eat fifty chicken wings. He did a lot of chewing, licking his fingers, and talking with his mouth full, all behavior I can watch at my own dinner table and without the commercials. He didn't get all fifty down, though to his credit he did eat a lot of wings. I know because I traded part of a precious Saturday afternoon to watch him do it. I could have been eating my own chicken wings.

I saw a man try and fail to beat the Guinness World Record for placing watermelons on another man's bare stomach, then chopping them in half with a large sword. You might be better informed than I am, but up until that moment, I had no idea there was such a record. Thankfully the man never chopped his volunteer in half. It really would have slowed him down if he'd had to find a new one for every watermelon.

There's plenty of dumb stuff on other screens too. Just today a Facebook friend posted photos of her birthday party including several shots of drunken behavior—her own. I hope her parents don't see those. Or her kids.

And every time I open my newsfeed I'm greeted with inane headlines like, "This Question Will Tell You if You're a Psychopath" and "Ice-T Reveals He's Never Eaten this Food and the Internet Totally Freaks Out," proving what I've known all along: some people have too much time on their hands and should come paint my house. Unless they're psychopaths.

Oh, and by the way, it's bagels. It's true. As of this writing, Ice-T has never eaten a bagel. Yes, I read the article, but just to save you the trouble.

The other thing that happens when you spend too much time watching screens is you start believing commercials. You start thinking alcohol will make you smarter and teeth can never be too white.

The sound on the television was turned down when I saw an infomercial for doublewide lawn chairs. There was a shot of the doublewide lawn chairs; then a shot of the doublewide lawn chairs in different colors; then a shot of people wearing sunglasses, smiling and sitting on the doublewide lawn chairs; then a shot of different people wearing sunglasses, smiling and sitting on different-colored doublewide lawn chairs, then all of it all over again. If I'd turned the sound up, they might have convinced me that life is more fun if you have doublewide lawn chairs. But sitting there with the sound off, I interpreted the commercial to mean that we're going to need doublewide lawn chairs if we sit on our fannies all day watching infomercials.

You may even start talking—or singing—in advertising slogans if you spend too much time screen-side.

Once when my son was very young, he and his friend sang "viva Viagra" from the backseat of my car, all the way across town. One morning after I hadn't slept well, he suggested I try Lunesta. Every time he popped a stick of gum in his mouth, he'd rave about minty freshness. But I first became interested in Screen-Free Week the day he told me he'd just saved a lot of money on car insurance.

The problem is when technology is on, we're off. We're not exercising, unless you count jumping up to run to the refrigerator every time there's a commercial. We're not spending quality time with our families. It's not bonding just because our butts are all bonding to the same couch.

And it's not communicating, at least not with

anyone in the room. I had ten people packed into my living room recently, and four of them were staring at screens of one kind or another. I wanted to say, "Hey, I'm your Facebook friend, and I'm standing right here!" I didn't though because I was afraid they'd unfriend me.

When I go out to dinner with my family and they stare at their cellphones, I want to take mine out, call one of them and ask, "Is this a good time to talk?"

Once, sitting across the table from my husband at a local restaurant, I couldn't figure out why he was pouting. Normally he doesn't act this way during dinner unless I've done the cooking.

"Are you upset about something?" I asked enough times that if he weren't upset before, he would be soon enough.

But he stared straight ahead, silent. Or maybe not quite straight ahead. Maybe a little up and ahead. Aha. It wasn't me he was mad at. He was watching the television behind me, and his team was losing.

It's painful when your date takes his eyes off you during dinner to watch Case Keenum—or Taylor Swift. It's even worse to see something unappetizing on television while you're eating food you'll have to pay for later. Not that we don't pay for the food we eat at home. And not that we never see anything unappetizing there either.

But the wrong moment on *Criminal Minds* could inspire a hunger strike and that wouldn't be good for the restaurant business. Once at a local dining establishment, our food arrived just as a documentary about giving birth came on television. I'm as amazed at the miracle of birth as anyone is, but I don't care to watch it while I eat nachos.

Why, I wonder, do we go to restaurants that serve TV with their entrees? It's not like we can hear what's on. We can't hear each other either. And we don't even get to control the remote which, by the way, should be a lesson to women everywhere. See! Contrary to what your husband has always told you, he can sit through an entire hour of television without once changing the channel.

Besides, it's not healthy to stare at a screen while you eat. You could miss a fly in your soup during a really good game or choke on your sandwich while you're yelling at the referee. And it can't be good for your digestion to watch a boxing match or a spaghetti western while you're eating…spaghetti. If restaurant televisions were all tuned to cooking shows, they would probably improve appetites, but

I'm not sure sports bar customers would go for it.

If you must do something while you watch television or stream movies, don't eat. Do something monotonous. File your nails, iron, mend—though I don't recommend you take your ironing or your mending to a restaurant. Probably not your nail file either.

These are exactly the types of activities television was made for. I tell my family that TV was designed specifically for people who are incapacitated, incarcerated or folding their laundry. They don't believe me, partly because they don't think laundry needs to be folded.

"But think what you're doing," I say. "Sitting on the couch, watching other people live fake lives while yours is passing you by." This line of reasoning always inspires them to nod dumbly and ask if I've seen the remote.

I don't spend eight and a half hours staring at screens and if I did I wouldn't admit it. I'm sure you don't either. But you may be worried about how the people in your life are going to spend the sixty extra hours they'll have if they participate in Screen-Free Week, not to mention the twelve to fifteen hours they'll save not looking for their iPad or the remote.

You could encourage them to be more physically active. They could go for walks, ride a bike—even clean the house. And if that doesn't use all their extra time, they could come clean mine.

They could volunteer. I've got some yard work they could do too.

If they want entertainment, they could turn on the radio and stare at it for a really long time. I'm joking. But they could read actual books. Then when you turn the television back on, they'll be better at *Jeopardy.*

They point is, during Screen-Free Week, we could all do things instead of watching other people do things. Instead of *Dancing with the Stars*, we could go dancing ourselves. Instead of watching *This Old House,* we could do our own home remodeling projects. And instead of watching *Barefoot Contessa,* we could go barefoot ourselves.

CHAPTER TWO

Be Glad You Can't Take It with You

Happy Simplify
Your Life Week!

The first week in August was named Simplify Your Life Week by some optimistic soul who wanted to encourage the rest of us to de-clutter and get organized. It's certainly a noble idea, but I'm afraid it's going to take most of us more than a week.

Where do you even start? I'll tell you right now; looking for advice on the fount of all wisdom, the internet, is no way to simplify your life. I got distracted reading about the ten best states to retire to, fad diets everyone should avoid and the most attractive celebrity gardens. Judging by the photos, celebrities get dressed up to work in the garden. That can't simplify life much.

Meanwhile frittering away the evening on the internet kept me from doing the supper dishes. Day-old dirty dishes don't simplify life either. I did find plenty of advice though, and it appears that if we really want to simplify our lives we have to get better at two things: managing our stuff and managing our time.

Let's start with managing our stuff because it directly impacts how much time we have to manage. I read that the average American spends 153 days of their life searching for misplaced belongings—car keys, shoes, homework. There are days I can't find my sofa.

Being above average, I've already used my 153 days, and quite possibly yours as well. I'd like to keep my remaining time free for more important activities, so after a great deal of research, I've collected the following rules, all based on the simple premise that we lose stuff because we have too darn much of it. It is, after all, easier to find a needle in a haystack then in a hayfield, though your odds aren't good either way.

1. If you don't desperately need it or absolutely love it, don't buy it. This would seem to include plastic fruit and lava lamps. If it's too late and you already have it, don't keep it. Unload it on someone who hasn't read my advice. It should be fairly easy to find someone like that.

2. If you don't use it, lose it. I misunderstood this the first time I read it, and I lost a whole lot of things before I realized that "lose it" means "get rid of it." I guess that just doesn't have the same ring to it.

3. When you bring something new into your home, get rid of something old. You should probably make an exception with children—though not with spouses.

4. If you need something, borrow it rather than buy it. This saves both storage space and money, though it can wreak havoc with your relationships.

5. Choose items you can use for more than one purpose. Forget the old adage about using the right tool for the right job. Anyone who has a high heel does not need a hammer, though a hammer doesn't double for a high heel as well. I don't have high heels, but I do have a set of five pounds weights and they make great hammers. I'm not sure how they work as weights.

6. You know you should have a place for everything and everything in its place, but did you know it's important to make it the same place every day? I won't mention any names, but someone I'm married to doesn't put things away. He puts them somewhere else—until he has time to put them away. (Or until I do it for him.)

If you have a similar system, you've probably discovered that when it's time to use a particular object, you've forgotten that you didn't put it in its proper place, although for many of us, that should be a given. When you don't find it there, you'll ask your spouse, "Where is it?" in that tone that really means, "Where did you put it?"

After a heated argument you'll remember that, as usual, you put it somewhere until you could get around to putting it away, which you never actually did. Then, not only will you have to apologize to your spouse; you'll have to look in all the places you normally put things until you have time to put them away. You can see how putting things in their proper place right away actually saves time, even if it means borrowing a ladder from the neighbor, carrying it across the street and up two flights of stairs and crawling into the attic to do it.

7. Consider a garage sale or mass giveaway when it's no longer possible for you to have a place for everything and everything in its place because you've run out of places. You may be tempted to add on to your home or even buy a new one when you find yourself in this situation. But be reasonable. It's one thing to buy a bigger house because you've had more children; it's quite another to buy a bigger house because you bought more shoes.

8. And finally, if after following all the rules you still manage to lose something important, don't spend more than ten minutes looking for it. Give up for now, trusting that it will eventually reappear, probably when you're looking for something else. Unfortunately, it could be years from now which may be too late to turn in your child's math homework.

Now let's move on to hints for managing your time, because if you follow all of my tips for managing your belongings you should have more of it. Theoretically anyway. I'll let you know if it's true after I start following my tips.

1. Keep a to-do list. I'm a great fan of lists, though I'm less a fan of doing what's on them. Still my to-do lists are so effective that sometimes I can use

the same one three or four days in a row.

2. Buy in bulk so you don't have to shop as often. As I'm sure you know, shopping is a great time suck. But be careful. I once purchased a dozen cans of beets because they were on sale. I thought I'd gotten a great deal right up until the moment I opened that first can. The beets were pickled. To my way of thinking, pickling is a waste of a perfectly good beet. A dozen cans of pickled beets can complicate your life for a long time if no one will eat them.

3. Cook in bulk and freeze meals. This saves both time and money. Keep in mind though, if you didn't like it the first time, chances are good you won't like it any better after it's been sitting in your freezer for a month and a half.

4. OHIO! Only Handle It Once. Deal with paperwork the minute you get it by tackling it, tossing it or filing it, and not just in Ohio.

5. Have a "launch site," a spot where you put everything you need to remember to take with you the next day. This could be in your entryway, on the corner of a table or right smack in front of the door, which will also serve to slow down any intruders. My launch site is the half-wall between our couch on the second floor and the stairs leading down to our front

door. And it really does simplify my life—until my car keys fall behind the couch.

6.   Simplify your wardrobe. I read that on a typical workday, the average women spends fourteen minutes deciding what to wear. That is the equivalent of two and a half days a year, and over the course of a career it totals four months she could be spending looking for lost objects.

I couldn't find the statistic for men, but I do know my husband doesn't spend that much time. And I think he could use the time he saves to simplify my life by making me breakfast while I'm deciding what to wear.

I think this last tip bears a bit more discussion—simplifying your wardrobe, not my husband cooking me breakfast, though that probably does as well. But simplifying our wardrobe perfectly illustrates how managing time and managing belongings comes together, often in a heap on the bedroom floor.

I personally have tried to simplify my wardrobe, and none too successfully thus far. I have three pairs of black pants, all of which I like, and three pairs of grey pants, none of which I like. I have a tee-shirt from every event I've participated in since seventh grade and a V-neck sweater I received as a gift in

1981. Mostly I wear just one pair of the black pants and one pair of the grey pants—never at the same time. I rarely wear tee-shirts, and I haven't worn the sweater in twenty years. I bet you wonder why I keep it. So do I.

Apparently, I'm typical. Average Americans wear only ten to twenty percent of their clothing. Our closets are like giant hope chests: storage for clothing items we *hope* will fit again someday. Or be in style again someday. Or learn to mend itself someday.

We could turn our bedrooms into thrift stores for people our size—and all the sizes we've ever been. Or we could rid ourselves of the eighty percent we never wear. My fashion consultant, Google, breaks it down into three steps.

1. Divide your clothing into four piles: *The Keep Pile:* These are your favorites. And right off I have a problem. My favorites are never in my closet. They're in the hamper, the laundry basket and the dryer. If it's in my closet, it probably isn't a favorite at all—and it could be more than thirty years old.

The Trash Pile: These are the clothes you're too embarrassed to donate. They're faded, stretched out or full of holes. I suggest you use them as rags or leave them on the doorstep of a quilter you know. Then ring the doorbell and run.

My ancient sweater still looks great. They don't make clothes that well anymore. I put it in the Keep Pile.

The Donate Pile: The experts say we should put all those items we haven't worn in the past year into a pile for donating. I assume that also means any item we haven't worn in the past twenty years. I move the sweater to the Donate Pile.

The Undecided Pile: Pack up the items you're not sure about and put them out of sight. If you miss something you can go retrieve it, but otherwise donate the whole box after three months. I've actually tried this step before—unsuccessfully. I peeked before I donated the box and wound up welcoming a few pieces back like they were old friends. In one particular case, I welcomed back a friend I've known since 1981.

2. Return everything from the Keep Pile to your now spacious closet. One expert suggests putting them back in "clusters," or groups of clothing that work together. This could shave a minute or two off decision time in the morning and also ensure

that you'll look well put together no matter what time you roll out of bed in the morning.

3. Now vow to maintain your newly cleaned and organized closet. As we've already established, when you get something new you should part with something old. Maybe the next time I get a new sweater, I'll finally get rid of a certain old one.

A Place for Every Doohickey and No Doohickey in Its Place

There comes a moment in the life of every family when someone declares it's time to downsize. Usually this is the parent with the fewest belongings.

Other family members don't always react enthusiastically to the suggestion so the inspired parent appeals to their higher motives. "Wouldn't it be nice to give away the things we don't need any more to people who do need them?" No one is persuaded, partly because they think they still need pretty much everything, and what they don't need, they want.

She tries another tack. She tells them she read that Americans spend more than sixty hours each year trying to find belongings in their homes. She points out that it might be easier to find what they need if they didn't have to wade through so much of what they don't need. "Just think, another sixty hours to play."

"But," the children argue, "We won't have anything left to play with."

She appeals to their baser motives. She suggests they sell everything they don't need—or want—at a garage sale and make some extra cash. "To buy more!" says a child enthusiastically.

And that settles it. They begin sorting their possessions optimistically, dollar signs in their eyes. But then they come across items they'd forgotten they even owned and they remember with a pang how special these once were. They recall the adventure they were on when they bought the talking trout or the kindness of the person who gave them the Mickey Mouse waffle maker. How can they possibly part with it? Belongings that have been under the bed covered with dust bunnies are transferred to places of honor on crowded shelves.

Someone remembers reading that a ponytail

brunette Barbie made in 1959 is now worth more than $10,000. Suddenly a slightly balding doll with ink marks for jewelry becomes the college fund. They forget that the Barbie was still hermetically sealed in her original box. Their doll has been lying in the corner of the moldy basement for four years. Still, they wrap it in tissue paper and carefully place it on the top shelf of the linen closet.

Many other potential giveaways are foiled by those five little words: "I might need it someday." The instigator of the cleanup begins to panic. "If it was so darn useful, why has it been in the crawl space covered in spider webs since we moved in twelve years ago?"

The finder counters, "If I'd known we had it, I'd have been using it." This is how power cords for unknown devices, parts for long-lost gadgets, jars without lids and lids without bowls find their way back onto cluttered shelves. At least they're up off the floor—for now.

Other things are too important to throw away. What if the IRS wants to see the receipt for the computer keyboard purchased in 2014? Or what if the current owner of the car they sold five years ago wants to see its maintenance history? They decide to keep them for now—to throw away later.

By now the reorganization effort has completely degenerated. When the parents aren't looking, the children snatch broken toys from the trash. And when the children aren't looking, the parents grab the children's discarded toddler toys and tattered baby blankets from the giveaway box—for the grandkids.

In the end, all the hours, sweat and arguments result in one bag of trash and one small stack in the middle of the living room. Unfortunately it's not nearly enough for a garage sale. What to do?

They decide to store it until there's more.

I'm not judging. I've made a few very unsuccessful attempts at gaining control of the stuff in my home too. Exhibit A is a story I call, A Place for Every Doohickey and No Doohickey in Its Place.

It all started one day when I was overcome with the urge to straighten our junk drawer. Maybe it was because I was over-caffeinated or maybe it was because the drawer no longer closed. Whatever the reason, as I worked I was reminded that a friend once told me his family doesn't have a junk drawer. I asked him where they keep their dead batteries and broken toys. He replied that his family doesn't need a junk drawer because they have a place for everything and everything they have is in its place. "And you know where that is?" I asked.

Actually I have a place for everything too—and that's the junk drawer. (But if you can't find it there, check the junk closet or the junk garage.) Here is a partial list of what I found in our junk drawer:

- Several razor blades—exposed razorblades, which I now know from experience, are best not kept in the junk drawer.

- Seven rolls of tape. There are seven because whenever I can't find tape I assume it's because we don't have any, so I buy more.

- One guitar pick—but no guitar. I believe that is kept in the junk closet.

- Miscellaneous items such as instructions for operating a camera we no longer own, the warranty for my blinds, a lottery ticket dated three years ago, one 32-cent stamp, a piece of dental floss and three or four hundred paper-clips. I'd like to say the paper clips were all gathered in one container, but the only ones that were gathered were stuck together in a giant wad of poster putty.

Why do I have so much in my junk drawer? A better question is why do I keep it?

Some of the items are insurance. For example I found a key in my junk drawer. I'll probably never find out it what opens unless I throw it away. Then I'll stumble across the lock it's made to open which will be on something very important and it will be locked.

Similarly I found one doohickey and several thing-a-ma-jigs. Since I didn't know what they were, it was hard to determine what they did. So again I decided to keep them because I would almost certainly discover their very important purposes within minutes of discarding them.

In other cases it's simply naive optimism that keeps me holding on. I found a vacuum cleaner belt and was optimistic enough to think we would remember to check the junk drawer the next time one breaks.

I found the tops for a dozen pens in my junk drawer. I keep them in case I ever find the pens they go with—or lose the top to a dozen just like them.

There was a stack of cards in my junk drawer that, even without counting, I could tell was substantially short of fifty-two. I put them back in the drawer because I'm convinced that the twenty-seven that are missing will show up someday.

The vast majority of stuff in my junk drawer I keep just in case. Just in case I ever lose my key ring, I have thirty-four more in my junk drawer—but just one key. Just in case I ever need a rubber band, I kept 436 of them. I kept one paint sample just in case we ever paint our house again. I kept three puzzle pieces just in case I ever meet the family that bought all our puzzles at a garage sale.

I know exactly what you're thinking. You're thinking that I must have kept almost everything. But I couldn't have because the drawer now closes.

I have made attempts to restore order on a larger scale too. Witness Exhibit B, which I call the Home Office Jungle. Let me set the scene:

I find myself on my hands and knees under my computer desk holding the phone against my ear with my shoulder, while Mr. Patient Technical Support Guy waits for me to determine if my modem is plugged in. I sincerely hope it is. You feel foolish when a repairman tells you the equipment isn't working because it's not plugged in. I do anyway.

But determining if our modem is unplugged is harder than you'd think. Turns out there's a jungle behind my home computer; a tangle of cords connecting hard drive, printer, speakers, monitor, keyboard, lamp, power strip, telephone, electric mixer, coffeemaker and blender. Yes, I'm exaggerating; we don't own a coffeemaker.

Starting at the modem, I try to follow the cord to the power strip, but three times I get lost in the tangle and have to start over. Then I bump my head, drop the phone and swear out loud before remembering this call is being monitored for quality assurance purposes. I finally determine that the cord is indeed plugged in. Mr. Patient Technical Support Guy says, "Yeah, I figured that would be too easy." Easy?

It turns out that the jungle behind my computer is only slightly worse than the jungle in front of and to the sides of my computer. So after we replace the modem, my husband and I decide our home office needs more room.

Here's something you should never do. You should never move your guestroom to your child's bedroom, your child's bedroom to your home office, and your home office to your guestroom. And if you do, you'd better hope you don't have any guests coming for a very long time.

The thought of unplugging all those cords behind the computer and plugging them in elsewhere was as appealing to me as carrying my four-drawer filing cabinet down two flights of stairs. So I ask my husband to do it. I also ask my husband and son to move all the furniture, which is what husbands and sons are for. I supervise, which is what I'm for.

Then I go to work in the corner beside the computer. We gave away our first few computers years ago, but we've maintained a shrine to them, made up of all their manuals, operating discs, cords and miscellaneous accessories. If the people we gave the computers to can get along without it all for this long, I figure we can too.

After clearing out the shrine, I start in on the filing cabinet and desk. It seems to me that before we can move them, it would be wise to clean them off, file what must be filed and toss what can be tossed. That includes coupons for products I don't use, bills that were paid long ago and warranties for items I'm not sure we even own any more.

It turns out our financial life is more complicated than it is successful. My husband, son and I bank at three different banks, and each one has changed names at least once, without our permission or input. Several different investment companies hold our retirement and college savings. And all of these have been sold or for other reasons changed their names, some more than once. The ensuing confusion has led to lackadaisical filing in our home. Well, something has led to lackadaisical filing in our home and that's what I prefer to blame it on.

I'm afraid, as I'm moving all the paper from the old office to the new one, that I'll misplace something important like the title to our car or a large sweepstakes check. And I must have because I can't find any large sweepstakes checks.

Even worse, I worry I might find something I've been living in blissful ignorance of, something that should have been dealt with long ago like a light bill or a subpoena.

I wade through this disaster before taking on the various knick-knacks and this-and-thats sitting around the office. I find it easier to give things away rather than throw them away. So I pack all but a few into boxes to be donated to someone who will probably throw them all away for me.

Technology is a great timesaver in all our lives, which is lucky because we need all the time we've saved to move and organize all our technology.

We have more power cords and chargers than we have electronic devices. This may be because we have chargers and power cords for electronic devices we no longer own. You may wonder why we keep them. We wonder why we keep them. But, I think it's for the same reason I kept that key in the junk drawer. The minute I discard it, I'll find out what it's for and it will be something very important. So just in case, we move all the power cords and chargers to the new office.

That leaves the miscellaneous stuff, the nitnoid bits and pieces of this and that. Every single piece of paper, every item of clothing and every thing-a-ma-bob has to be moved to its new location and put in its proper place, though "proper" may be too strong a word. Unlike my friend's family, we've never been one of those families with "a place for everything and everything in its place." It's more like "every-thing was someplace and now it's someplace else."

In the end we give away three boxes of stuff, throw away two bags of junk and put away the rest.

I had hoped I'd find a few things during what I'm now calling the Great Order Restoration Project: a favorite sweatshirt; a book from my childhood that I passed on to my son and haven't seen since; a pair of reading glasses, worn only once; and the key to our roll-top desk. It's a good thing we lost the key right after we bought the desk; we hadn't had time to lock it yet.

Unfortunately I don't find the key or any of those other things. But I did just misplace a flyswatter and another pair of reading glasses.

Be Glad You Can't Take It with You

I have a neat, uncluttered home. I have cleared away all the nonessential things in my life to make room for those that give me the most joy. I am a minimalist. And a liar.

What I really am is a minimalist wannabe, a minimalist trapped in a maximalist's life. That is, if by "minimalist" you mean "one who travels light through life." And if by "maximalist" you mean "one who has to clear off the dining room table to eat dinner, so she eats on the couch instead, but she has to clear that off too."

You may wonder why, in a culture where bigger is better and shopping is recreation, I aspire to minimalism—as though having to clear off the couch to sit down isn't reason enough. I've got plenty more:

1. My life is a mess when my stuff is a mess, and my stuff is a mess right now and has been for quite some time. It seems to me that one way to restore order to my stuff, and therefore my life, would be to have less stuff—less to clean, maintain, organize and track down when it goes missing, which it often does.

2. It's easier to enjoy what we have when we don't have so darn much of it—if only because we'll be able to find it. One Christmas Eve I watched a relative's five-year-old daughter unwrapping gift after gift. It was like Santa's sleigh had tipped over in the living room.

Finally, with many more presents still in need of unwrapping, the child threw up her hands and said, "Could I just play now?" I wanted to tell her parents that Jesus Christ himself only received three Christmas presents, and his mother was probably thinking, "Now what are we going to do with these?" The family was traveling at the time, after all.

3. We own our stuff or our stuff owns us. If you spend too much time cleaning, polishing or in other

ways maintaining an item, it owns you. That's why I don't clean my house; it needs to know who's in charge.

4. More isn't always better. More is just… well…more—more for the trash bin, more for the storage unit, more for the next garage sale. By the way, a garage sale is nothing more than a place to sell all the stuff we don't need in order to make room for different stuff we don't need.

5. It isn't he who has the most who wins; it's she who wants the least. In the end we can't take any of it with us anyway, which is lucky because having to haul it around for all eternity would be hell. And we really can't take it with us. No one ever does. They leave it for someone else to deal with. And still we never learn.

If you're ever tasked with cleaning out your parents' home, I can almost guarantee that as you're working you'll be repeating the following mantra: "I will never do this to my children. I will never do this to my children." And while you're chanting, you'll be filling boxes with everything you want to keep.

I can also guarantee that one day your kids will have to sort through it, along with your other belongings, all the while saying, "I will never do this to my children. I will never do this to my children."

It's the cycle of life—or the cycle of stuff. And I went through it myself. I'm grateful my parents weren't exactly collectors. But neither were they disposers. There's a fine distinction. They didn't buy what they didn't need, but they didn't get rid of what they no longer needed either. And they had an amazing talent for fitting a lot into a small home. The fact that they raised ten children in a three-bedroom house should give you some indication of just how good they were at it.

As is usually the case, I have some advice for you if you're facing this daunting project.

1. Put together a team of people with a variety of talents to help you. Just make sure they're all on speaking terms. No sense in coming to blows over the family treasures, some of which might be breakable. Fortunately, my siblings and I get along wonderfully. It's something you learn to do when there are ten of you packed into a three-bedroom house. Or maybe it's sharing one bathroom that does it.

If you're lucky, you'll have one team member who is extremely organized. We did, and it wasn't me. You should also have someone who is strong and willing to carry boxes. We did, and that wasn't me either.

There should also be a nice balance of sentimentality and practicality in your group. You don't want anyone tossing your grandmother's nearly 100-year-old wedding dress. But you don't want to save all the old Christmas cards and baby teeth either. Actually we didn't find any of those. My mom couldn't be sentimental about baby teeth when there were so many of them.

Finally, it might be helpful to have a team member with practical knowledge about the value of heirlooms. They can reassure any regular viewers of *American Pickers* you have in your group that you aren't discarding anything worth millions.

This wasn't an issue for us. The bigger the family the less the likelihood of there being anything valuable in the home. Large families tend to spend their money on more important things like, for example, groceries. You can have a lot of money or you can have a lot of children. You can't have both—unless you have your own reality show. And now that I think about it, cleaning out family homes might make a good one. I can't believe no one has thought of that yet.

2.   Identify organizations and individuals who may want your castoffs. It's hard to part with things that have been in the family for decades, even if you don't need them. You'll feel better about it if you can give them away to someone else who doesn't need them either.

3.   Pass the buck. You're bound to come across some items you've done without for years, even forgot existed, but one look and you won't be able to discard them. So don't. My mother kept much of our childhood artwork as well as every dumb thing we ever made for her. And when you have ten children, that's a lot of dumb things. We couldn't bring ourselves to dispose of it all. So we sorted it into boxes, one for each sibling. They can throw it away themselves if they want to. Or their kids can.

Get a Free Glass with Every Drink You Have at My House

Do you ever worry that after you're gone, your children and grandchildren will snoop through your home searching for heirlooms, and they'll open a cupboard and be knocked to the ground by all the junk you've collected over the years? Then they'll realize that, just as they'd suspected all along, you really were quite unstable and they should probably go ahead and contest your will. You don't worry about that? I do, and for good reason.

People looking through my home now think I'm

unstable. Recently a friend reached into my kitchen cupboard for a glass and burst out laughing. "You're a collector!"

Naturally I denied it. The way I see it, there are collectors and there are disposers. Collectors spend their lives gathering items for their estate sale. Disposers spend their lives giving stuff away. Usually they marry each other.

But even as I protested my friend's accusation, I realized that not only are my husband and I *both* collectors, we're the worst kind of collectors: the accidental kind. True collectors are driven by their interests. Most of what we've collected has come to us the way litter collects in a road ditch and tumbleweeds gather on a chain link fence.

I certainly didn't set out to collect drinkware. And yet along with our set of ordinary drinking glasses, we have a fancy set we never use and a dozen canning jars we do use, but not for canning. We also have a dozen plastic cups from convenience stores all over town. As an ardent recycler, I love that they can be refilled and I'd love it more if I remembered to take one with me when I go to a convenience store.

Rounding out our glass collection are the dozen or so beer and wine glasses with logos from the establishments they came from. Apparently paying more for a drink so you can keep the glass it came in is seen as a good deal by people who've been drinking.

Unfortunately, glasses aren't the only things that have collected in our home. Some things we keep because I'm afraid my husband will notice if I try to get rid of them. He buys a new baseball cap everywhere we travel, not because he collects them but because he forgot to bring one with him when we left home. We have more caps than the American League.

Some things we keep because they could be worth money someday. We have a veritable alphabet soup of entertainment: cassettes, LPs, CDs, VHS tapes and DVDs. I'm just thankful we don't have any eight-track tapes—that I know of. They could be around here somewhere.

A few things we keep are worth money now. We have so many coupons that in order to use them all, I'd need to purchase an elaborate filing system and hire an assistant to organize it. And that might defeat the purpose.

A lot of things we keep because we may need them someday. Chargers and power cords have taken over our home like bindweed. But I'm afraid to get rid of any of them because I'm not sure what they're all for.

I have a bag full of widowed socks, some whose partners were probably lost in our last home. I'm afraid if I toss any of them, their partners will show up shortly thereafter, having taken nineteen years to walk the six blocks from my old neighborhood.

I hate to admit it, but I keep a lot of things because I have a sentimental streak. For example, I have scrapbooks from my college days, and I didn't just go to college yesterday. Along with the usual ticket stubs and fortunes from fortune cookies, my scrapbooks also contain page after page of small cardboard circles taken off the top of a particular brand of yogurt. If you're ever snooping through my home, you might question why I saved those. I do too. At least I know that at one point in my life I was getting plenty of calcium.

I keep a variety of inspirational quotations and messages meant to motivate me to become the person I want to be. If you stumbled across them, you might be curious what kind of person that is especially since I've doctored a few of them. For example, there's the one that says, "You are what you think about." I sincerely believe that, but somewhere along the way I added, "So stop thinking about Cheetos."

I have a file cabinet filled with scraps of paper containing cryptic handwritten notes intended for use in future writing projects. Out of context these may seem peculiar to anyone who comes across them—even in context they might seem peculiar. For example, "It's almost impossible to eat soup while reclining," and "We've all got our talents. Mine is hindsight."

I even have a file filled with rejections from editors. Rejections are kind of a badge of honor for a writer—a badge with a big pin that stabs you right in the heart but a badge nonetheless. If you snoop around my house very long, you're bound to discover that more editors have said no to me than have said yes. Unfortunately you will have no way of knowing those who said yes are smarter. Probably better looking too.

Also we keep some things because we've forgotten we even have them. We rarely open the cupboard that contains all our cookbooks and coffee mugs. Anyone snooping through my house would wonder why I have so many cookbooks when I cook the same six meals over and over and why we have so many mugs when we don't even drink coffee. I suppose they'll come in handy if we ever run out of glasses.

I also want to express my frustration at the many well-meaning businesses and organizations that are contributing to what you, if you've read this far, can see is a severe case of TMC—Too Much Crap—in my home and probably yours too.

My husband and I both have entire drawers of T-shirts we rarely wear. My son has a similar drawer and he doesn't even live with us anymore. That's because we've all received T-shirts for every single event we've ever participated in. I wear T-shirts to exercise in, but I don't exercise that much and when I do I only wear one shirt.

If we don't get T-shirts we get water bottles. And sometimes we get both. When both my son and I got braces, we were each given drawstring backpacks containing T-shirts, water bottles and an assortment of other smaller gifts meant to advertise the orthodontist's business and make us feel better about wearing braces. It didn't. I wanted to ask them to keep everything and deduct the cost of it all from our bill.

We have a stack of address labels sent to us by organizations who think we'll be so grateful that we'll put one of those return address labels on an envelope, address it to them and stick a check inside. Too bad for them; we're not that grateful. In fact we're annoyed. We have so many address labels now that we'll never be able to move.

We have a refrigerator covered in magnets that have been given to us. The magnets, not the refrigerator. We bought that.

We have a closet full of fleece blankets mailed to us by a nonprofit we gave to once a long time. They'd be perfect for baby blankets but we don't have a baby. And the nonprofit long ago used up our donation making and mailing us all those blankets.

I'm all for free gifts but honestly, I'd be happier with five dollar bills. They're so much more practical.

To be fair, businesses do give us some things we need. We just don't need quite so many of them. (Also "give" probably isn't quite the right word.)

We have a collection of canvas bags that, like the T-shirts, advertise the fine businesses that gave them to us. We have piles of both the useful flat-bottom bags that are good for grocery shopping and the kind without the flat bottoms that aren't good for anything.

You may wonder why, if I have so many canvas bags, I also have an entire drawer full of plastic grocery bags. I'll tell you why. Even a sturdy, flat-bottom canvas bag is only good for grocery shopping if you remember to bring it to the store.

At least I can use the plastic grocery bags for trashcan liners. I can't use the giant plastic bags I get at the dry cleaners at all. Every time I have dry cleaning done, I get a bag and a new set of wire hangers. I have no use at all for gigantic plastic bags with holes in both ends. And while we do use the hangers, we now have more hangers than we have clothes—partly because hangers never stop fitting.

We have enough plastic cups from convenience stores and fast food restaurants to host our entire neighborhood for iced tea. And if we ever do, we'll let them keep the cups.

I have so many name badges and neck wallet lanyards from conferences I've attended that I'm thinking of hosting my own conference. I'm not sure what we'll confer about yet, but I do know that all the participants will get a lanyard, a water bottle and a T-shirt. Maybe a stack of wire hangers too.

Truly I dream of a BYO world. Bring your own canvas bag. Bring your own hanger. Bring your own glass—except when you come to my house. I've got one for you.

Dear Santa, Please Bring Socks

Fifteen years have gone by, but I'm still haunted by a memory from my son's childhood. We were at a fast food restaurant and he was out of earshot when I ordered his meal. "You could get a kid's meal for him," said the young woman behind the counter.

"No thank you," I whispered.

"It's cheaper."

"I don't want a kid's meal."

"You get a toy with it."

"I don't want a toy."

"But...."

"Look! I will pay you extra to keep the toy."

"Huh?"

"I can't close my purse because I have a Pokémon and six cars in it. I stepped on a bite-sized T-rex when I got out of bed this morning. I don't want a toy! And don't ask me again or I'll take my ten dollars and go somewhere else!"

I'm not sure but I may have had her by the collar by then.

My son ate his supper happily, unconcerned by his lack of toy and the scene it had caused. I congratulated myself for taking control. Or so I thought.

We were nearly finished when a mother with three young children in tow marched over to my table. Without asking my permission or that of her children, she thrust all three of her children's unopened kid's meal toys into my son's hands. "We don't need any more of these," she said.

He said, "Thank you."

I said, "But...but...but...."

May the scoundrel who invented kid's meal toys step on a plastic T-rex too. May he be forced to eat at fast food restaurants every single meal for the rest of his sorry life. May his grandchildren and great grandchildren throw tantrums in public places, begging him for the remaining twenty-three of the next item he promotes with "Collect all 24."

Children love kid's meal toys—for ten minutes. That's because a toy gives them something to do while they're supposed to be eating the lunch you just bought them. Beyond that I never actually saw my child play with one. I didn't mind that he forgot about them, I just wished he would have done it sooner—like before we left the restaurant.

But kid's meal toys were only part of the toy infestation in our home. Like all children mine was a magnet for material things. When he was very young, I recognized every miniature vehicle he owned, and if he started to leave one behind at a friend's home, I could remind him. Eventually miniature vehicles filled an entire box in his bedroom—a large box. I could no longer recognize them all, and even if I could have, I wouldn't have reminded him if he left one behind.

He would never have agreed, but I thought he needed more toys like Bill Gates needed more money. I landed on Legos when I fell into bed at night. I stepped on little green army men when I dragged out of bed in the morning. For years after we gave Mr. Potato Head away, we found his body parts all over the house.

As the years went by, toys in our home got smaller and the collections got larger. There were model building supplies, Legos and airsoft pellets everywhere—in the couch cushions, under the beds, in the dishwasher. It was like having a bad case of ants.

People without children will say naively, "Well stop buying toys." But modern parents don't have to buy toys; toys find children, and not just at fast food restaurants. Snack foods and other food items come packaged with toys. Toys are an incentive to sell cookie dough, wrapping paper and all manner of other fundraising items. Parents would prefer a commission. That way we could be reimbursed for the gas used on sales calls.

My son's dentist gave him toys after every visit. Why couldn't he just pass out candy like my dentist did when I was growing up?

Before parents know what hits us, toys have taken over our homes like germs in a daycare. And as parents we know that quality toys serve a purpose. They allow kids to play creatively and remain occupied while we stare at our smartphones. But we can't help but fear we're raising little materialists who think it's normal to get another new toy every other day.

Now that I'm an empty nester, I've had time to consider how I might have done things differently. If you still have young children, try my new five-step plan to decrease the number of toys in your home.

1. Just before Christmas, instruct your children to give away an agreed-upon number—maybe fifty to a hundred. I'm kidding. They probably won't agree to that many. But try telling them that their beloved toys will be in the hands of less fortunate children who will love them as much as they did. If that doesn't work, remind them that Christmas is coming and they need to make room. If that doesn't work, sort through the toys yourself while they're sleeping.

2. Encourage friends and relatives to give functional gifts, such as money for the college fund or socks and underwear. Those are always a hit with children.

3. Re-gift. During the frenzy of opening gifts, snatch a few of the new toys, rewrap them and set them aside for the next birthday party your child is invited to. Be prepared though. Later they may ask where these toys are. This is a teachable moment,

and that's why you should lie. Say in your sternest parent voice, "With as many toys as you have, it's no wonder you can't find them."

4.   Refuse kid's meal toys at fast food restaurants. You could even order adult meals for your children and then eat their leftovers.

5.   There are certain toys you must ban entirely from your home. These include toys that promote violence or disrespect and any that say anywhere on the packaging, "Collect all twelve!"

CHAPTER THREE

Under Attack

A World without Patience

Some people pray for patience. I pray for a world where I don't need any. And I wouldn't need any if I were never on hold—which I am right now. Again.

I've spent half my life on hold. At least I've spent half my day on hold. I must have; a recorded message has come on the phone two or three hundred times to say, "Thank you for your patience. A customer service representative will be with you shortly." She's giving me more credit than I deserve. My lack of patience is legendary. So is my tendency to exaggerate.

But I wouldn't need patience at all if I were never on hold. Or if I were never trapped in one of those voicemail mazes, punching this number and that number and pleading with a recorded message, "Please, could I just talk to a real person?"

And I wouldn't need patience if I never had to remember another password, if my name were enough. Most days I can remember that.

And I wouldn't need patience if I weren't interrupted every eighteen minutes by phone calls from the IRS and the Resort Rewards Center. Apparently I won a cruise and I'll be arrested for tax fraud the minute I get off the ship.

And if I didn't open my email every day to spam messages like the one I got today: "You can be a medical doctor in less time than you think." That's all we need—doctors with less education.

"Thank you for your patience. A customer service representative…"

What patience? If I had patience, I wouldn't have just told Silicon Sally that I'd like another recorded message to take over for her, because if I have to hear her voice one more time I'll reach through the phone and pull her tonsils out. She didn't hear me, which is okay. I don't think she has tonsils anyway.

My pittance of patience would be enough if I never had to return a product, but if I wanted to, it would fit back in the box it came in. And if sleeping bags fit into their sacks as slick as greased pipe fittings, only without the grease.

I wouldn't need patience if political campaigns were a lot shorter. And if there were no fleas, ticks or mosquitoes and whatever important role they play in the great web of life were carried out by critters that are cuter and don't bite.

And if I never misplaced anything. But on the off chance I did, everything I own would have a locater button like my old cordless phone did. That includes my car keys, my sunglasses and the lid to my food processor.

"Thank you for your patience. A customer service representative…"

What patience? If I had patience, I'd have found the lid before I tried to use my food processor.

And I wouldn't need patience if cling wrap didn't cling to itself. And if hot dog buns came in packages of ten like hot dogs do. And if my water heater never gave me the cold shoulder. And if all appliances were self-cleaning. So were toilets. And houses.

I wouldn't need patience if there were no such

thing as post-nasal drip. And if my arms were long enough to scratch my back. And if my head were flat so that it would be easier to sleep on my back when I don't have a pillow handy.

I wouldn't need patience if the chocolate coating on ice cream bars didn't break off and fall on my shirt. What? We can put a man on the moon, but we can't have ice cream bars that don't shed?

"Thank you for your patience…"

Blah, blah, BLAH! I'll thank you to stop saying that! I ran out of patience long ago and I wouldn't need it if someone would answer this phone.

And I wouldn't need patience if people would stop leaving their grocery carts in the middle of the parking lot. And if no one ever spit their gum on the sidewalk. But if they did, they'd be the one who stepped on it.

And if I could read our insurance and retirement information without getting a law degree.

And if spellcheckers and autocorrect software could read my mind so I would never again tell someone "the launch is on" when I mean "the lunch is at one."

And if the owners of dogs that bark all night could hear them as well as the rest of us do. And if everyone else followed traffic rules and overlooked it when I forget to.

And if no one ever used the last paper towel without refilling it or put an empty milk jug back in the refrigerator. What do they think? There's a cow in there?

"Thanks for waiting. How can I help you?"

Patience, smatience. I wouldn't need patience if fitted sheets were easier to fold. And if ...what?

Keep It Down!

I was given a free cowbell at the minor league hockey game I attended recently. I asked if I could have a free hot dog instead since I don't have any cows at home. But I was told that true hockey fans show their enthusiasm by ringing cowbells during the game. I'm not sure why; I grew up in cattle country and I never once saw cows playing hockey.

I will say the game was worth getting noisy over. If I were the type to ring a cowbell in the ear of the person sitting in front of me, I would have done it. But I stuck the cowbell in my coat pocket and watched the game with my hands over my ears.

To say I might be a little sensitive to noise is like saying you might be a little sensitive to poison ivy.

I like quiet and it's not because I'm getting old, though I am getting old. Maybe it's because I'm a mom and because I was raised in a three-bedroom home with nine siblings. I've been deprived of peace and quiet my entire life. Whatever the reason, too much racket makes me irritable, and you don't want to see me irritable.

I tolerate our snow blower because my husband operates it and we have the windows closed when he does it. Also because it beats shoveling. But when he talks about getting a leaf blower, I draw the line. Those are so noisy and why do we need one? We have wind.

He also wants a motorcycle. Whenever he mentions it, I remind him of that hearing-impaired biker we met once. My husband said to the guy, "Nice bike." And the biker said, "Nice to meet you Mike." That didn't really happen but I still remind him of it.

See how noise brings out the worst in me? And it's not just the big things. We start our days with a buzz from the alarm, and we finish it with the clamor of the nightly news. In between we have a relentless assortment of gratuitous dings, rings, clings and clangs. It's like having high-tech hailstones landing on a tin roof all day long.

A man I know told me his watch alarm started beeping in the middle of a church service. Everyone could hear it—except him. He's a little hard of hearing, which is just as well because he didn't know how to turn it off anyway.

A coworker of mine sets her watch to beep when it's time to go home at the end of the workday. This is amazing to me since I've never once had to be reminded. I know people who set their watches to prompt them when it's time to break for lunch. If they can forget to eat how can they be trusted with anything else?

My car dings when I'm about to leave the lights on, lock up my car keys or run out of gas. It dinged at me all the way across town yesterday because the box sitting on my passenger seat refused to put on its seatbelt.

At the gas pump there's a beep to remind me to choose how I'll pay for the gas (inside, outside, credit, cash or first born). There's another beep to remind me to punch in my choice of gas (expensive, very expensive or have mercy on us) and finally there's a beep to remind me to pay the cashier. There's just one little beep between me and petty theft.

Cellphones distract me during funerals and awaken me during meetings. And "ring" doesn't begin to describe what phones do these days. They sing, beep and buzz. They chirp, trill, chime and vibrate. It's like a new species of bird has migrated into the area.

Some of us have our phones set to ping every time we get an email, and since even the smartest smartphone can't distinguish between a message from a friend and one from the Nigerian Oil Ministry, they ping a lot. They buzz to remind us of appointments and deadlines. We might still be late, but we always feel guilty at the right time.

They chirp to tell us we have a tweet or a Facebook message, and they ring, ding or play a rousing chorus of "La Bamba" every time we get a phone call.

We can have practically any type of music, from classical to jazz to mariachi serenade everyone at the movies. We can interrupt our next meeting with our choice of animal sounds: a chimpanzee, a wolf howling or a dog—not barking but laughing. I've heard it. It sounds like Old Yeller in the front row of a comedy club. And after all that, I still had to listen to the cellphone owner's conversations. Well, I didn't have to, but I did.

We can download a ringtone that sounds like Yogi Bear repeating, "I got a text and you didn't." Or one of an angry fellow yelling, "Pick up the phone! Would you please pick up the phone? Pick it up! Pick it up! PICK IT UP," which is exactly what everyone in earshot is thinking.

We can have a ringtone of a baby laughing which is probably better than a baby crying. Or we can download one that wolf whistles at us every time we get a call. That could be a real self-esteem booster.

All of these are entertaining the first time we hear them but much less so after four or five hundred times. If we don't silence our phones, we run the risk of someone doing it for us...with a hammer.

And the odds are good that eventually our clever ringtone will go off at the wrong time sometime. More than once I've heard cellphones ring while I was doing a presentation, and one of those times I was in the middle of a joke about cellphones. I'm not making that up. I hate to admit it, but the joke was a lot funnier when the phone rang.

I was at a banquet where a cellphone rang at the head table during an award presentation. To make matters worse, it belonged to the honoree's mother, and she missed much of the presentation while she tried to locate and silence her phone. So did the rest of us. Fortunately, the ringtone was a little musical ditty and not, "Pick it up! Pick it up! PICK IT UP!"

I've heard cell phones go off during church services many times, but the worst was when one rang just as its owner was about to receive communion. At least it wasn't a wolf whistle or a mariachi band.

I'm not judging—or planning to tell you about all the times I've neglected to silence my own phone. I'm just explaining why I use a common boring ringtone. It's for all those times I forget.

The point is, it's no wonder I crave quiet. I love that Bible story where God tells the prophet Elijah to leave a cave and go stand on the mountain to meet Him. There was a big loud wind, but God wasn't in the wind. He wasn't in the fire or the earthquake either. But finally there was a gentle breeze. When Elijah heard it, he went out and stood in the entrance of the cave to meet God. The Bible doesn't say so, but I think he knew enough to leave his cellphone inside.

Leave Me Alone,
Elizabeth

I was loaded down like a pack mule. I had a purse so big it could double as a gym bag. I had my padfolio with papers poking out the edges. I had my lunch, an assortment of snacks and an iced tea the size of San Diego. You never know; I could get stranded during my five-minute commute to work.

But what was that? I stopped halfway down my stairway and listened. Was it…? Yes, it was. I'd been expecting a call and my cellphone was vibrating from the depths of my purse. It sounded like there was a giant fly trapped inside.

I put everything down on my steps to dig for my phone, and in the process I bumped my tea. It tumbled down the stairs, spraying the walls, the stairway and me. Ice cubes flew every which way. A few of them hit my cat and he bolted like he thought I was throwing things at him. I dove into my hand-bag and emerged wet and annoyed but victorious, my phone still buzzing.

I answered it expecting great things and…dang. It was her again. I'd spilled a gallon of iced tea, upset my cat and made myself late for work all so that I could take a call from the queen of phone scammers: Elizabeth from the Resort Rewards Center. And I would have known it was her—or Rachel from Card Services or Sam from Travel Promotions—if I had only looked at my cellphone before I answered it. Elizabeth was calling from a Madisonville, Tennessee phone number. I bet she doesn't live in Madison-ville, Tennessee. Neither does anyone else I know.

I don't have to look at my call history to know I get more phony phone calls than real ones—and by a wide margin. You'd think that, realizing this, I wouldn't be in such a rush to answer the phone. I would think so too.

I hung up and yelled at the phone in my hand, "I've about had it with you...you... you phony phoner!" And I have about had it. I'm afraid that one of these days, I'll hear a voice that reminds me of Elizabeth and I'll march up to some poor innocent stranger, grab her by the collar and scream "Leave me alone, Elizabeth!" And she'll say, "My name is Joan," and have me arrested.

Maybe I won't go that far. Maybe I'll just answer my next call and without waiting to find out who it is, I'll start ranting as only I can. If it's you calling, don't take it personally. Just stay on the line and murmur reassuringly until I calm down.

That could take a while. In fact, all the while I was mopping up iced tea, picking up ice cubes, changing my shirt, comforting my cat and driving to work late, I was muttering everything I'd like to say to Elizabeth, Rachel, Sam and the rest of them: "Isn't it bad enough that I spend half my work day sorting through junk mail and deleting spam emails. Now you're monopolizing the other half. I'm sure American productivity suffers because of the likes of you. I know mine does. And another thing; I was in an accident because of one of your kind." I wouldn't have to tell them it was an iced tea accident.

There are just so many phony phoners. If I didn't know better, I'd think I was becoming really popular. Suddenly people from all over the country are trying to contact me. Or at least the numbers look like they're from all over the country. Maybe leopards can't change their spots but skunks can change their stripes.

I'm not sure what they all want though, because I'm answering my phone less and less. Back in my landline days I answered all my phone calls politely and when I got one that sounded questionable, I'd say "She's not home. Can I take a message," as though I were the housekeeper. I knew it was deceitful. Anyone looking at our house would know we don't have a housekeeper. But at least I was courteous. And I don't think there's any ethical reason why you can't lie to a liar.

For a while I even answered every call I got on my cellphone. Well, except the ones I got in church. I didn't answer those.

But now I leave the ringer off and when my phone vibrates, I glance at the caller ID on the off chance that I might recognize the number. I rarely do, so these days I let most of my calls go to voice mail. Yes, I've been forced to screen my calls.

Apparently everyone else is doing it too, because no one takes my calls anymore either.

So Phone Scam Sam and Fraud Call Frannie now leave messages claiming they can lower my credit card interest rate or that I'm in trouble with the IRS. Recently I had a message warning me that there's been a warrant issued for my arrest in a town I've never visited. Unfortunately I've forgotten the name of the town. That's too bad because I probably should avoid it.

One day I lost my temper, picked up my vibrating phone and screamed into it, "Stop calling me!" It was a recording.

Still, it was oddly satisfying. The next time my phone rang, I didn't even wait for "hello." I told a caller to get a real job. It was my husband. I'm joking. It was a scammer. And I've never been the same.

A few days later I asked a caller if his mother knew what he did for a living. I told another that I'd give her my credit card number if she'd give me hers first. I held the phone away from my ear during one call and, as loud as I could whisper, said to the empty room, "I'll keep him on the line while you trace the call."

One day I even called a scam number back. When a real person answered, I stayed quiet while he said, "Hello, hello." Then I did it again—six times. To his credit, each time he answered in that polite way you do when you want to bilk someone out of their life savings.

It was rude and I'm not proud of it. But I'm not the only one who behaves badly in the face of bad behavior. A friend told me once that when a spam caller asked for her husband, she said he'd died recently and would therefore be unable to come to the phone. Meanwhile her healthy husband stood nearby, listening to her side of the conversation and wondering if he had anything to be worried about.

Another friend told me that when someone claiming to be her grandson called asking for bail money, she said, "Is that you, Michael?" The caller said, "Yes" and she said, "That's odd. My grandson's name isn't Michael."

I haven't gotten the fake grandchild call yet. It's a common scam though, so I'm rehearsing. I plan to tell my fake grandchild, "You're on your own this time. You still owe me from the last time I bailed you out!"

The experts say that you should hang up quickly when you realize it's a scammer calling. Do not engage. But I'm no expert.

They advise you to put your name on the Do Not Call Registry, which does stop calls from legitimate organizations you don't want to hear from. But I figure anyone who makes a career of grand theft won't be deterred by a little law forbidding calls to numbers on the Do Not Call Registry.

Still, you should listen to the experts. Don't behave like I have. I feel bad that I've let robo robbers and cuckoo callers bring out the worst in me—and confirm that my number works. But I can't stop myself.

Today I answered a call from a scammer, held my phone next to the wall and started knocking and saying in a mournful voice, "Let me out. Let me out." I could hear the scammer saying, "Hello… ma'am…hello." I was enjoying myself immensely until a coworker walked into my office and asked if I was okay.

No, probably not.

Waging War with
Dura Bowl

I sat down at my home computer one morning to check my email, and there were 41 new messages and 188 old messages dating back seven months. Those old emails have been bothering me like a guilty conscience. And the oldest one was from...well... me. I'd sent myself a message from work reminding me to change the furnace filter. I'm not sure I ever did it, but it's probably time to send another reminder anyway.

I don't know what came over me, but that morning

I dealt with every single message. I started with the low-hanging fruitcakes: the Viagra vendors and the rich widows desperately hoping to give me their money before they die.

Then I went through the rest. I responded, deleted, filed and got up and changed the furnace filter. Then I went back and responded, deleted and filed some more. After three long hours, I had an empty inbox. It was a beautiful thing. I sat and stared at the empty screen for a long time. I knew it wouldn't last because, while I may indeed suffer from email overload, I also have a severe case of email efficiency deficiency. In other words, my own bad habits are contributing to the e-buildup in my inbox.

For one thing I put off replying to certain messages because I think the sender deserves an especially thoughtful, eloquent response and it takes me a long time to come up with one of those. That means the more important the email, the longer I wait to answer it. Eventually time runs out and I'm forced to reply. I cannot tell you the number of thoughtful, eloquent emails that have been replaced by quick ones that would have been fine if they weren't two weeks late. For example, I received the message "I sincerely hope you can attend our gathering." My response was "How did it go?"

Not only that, I handle email like a bad story problem. "Dorothy receives seven emails, answers two, gets discouraged and closes down her computer. Later, while standing in line at the sub shop she checks her phone and sees she's received nine new messages. She answers three, gets to the front of the line and closes her email. She turns on her computer before bed and sees she's received twelve messages. She's too tired to deal with them so she closes her email and plays solitaire for half an hour. If Dorothy keeps this up, how long until her inbox is full?"

I also contribute to the email overload because I don't always read a message fully before responding. This forces the other person to send me another message—or two. For example, a friend writes, "What time will you be arriving? Can you bring the paper plates?" And I write back, "Sure."

Other times I don't ask enough questions. I recently participated in an email conversation that went something like this:

"What day works for you?"

"How about Monday?"

"Monday is out."

"How about Wednesday?"

"What time?"

"Eleven?"

"Won't work."

"How about 2?"

"Nope."

"CALL ME!"

"Why?"

I don't mean to imply that I'm entirely to blame for my email overload, however. Not by a long shot. I have now reached a point in my online existence where I'm receiving more spam than regular email. In fact, I'm receiving more spam than regular email, snail mail, phone calls and greetings on the street combined. I don't know how they did it, but they got to me. Track R Bravo, Dura Bowl, Easy Loans and a host of other unsavory characters got their cyber paws on my email address.

I've had the same address since email was invented, or at least since I got it. And I was very careful about sharing it. For years I got by with the occasional plea from a Nigerian widow or an invoice for a toll road I've never been on but then suddenly POW, a steady stream of e-rubbish! Amazing deals on everything from toilet paper to Alaskan tours. "Straight talk about hair transplants." "Boost your memory by 44 percent!" "Eat dessert daily and don't gain a pound!" I almost fell for that one.

Spammers offer me all sorts of free stuff like movie tickets, digital cameras, glucose meters and information on psoriasis, all of which are very hard to pass up. One even offered me fifty pounds of free lobster. But I ignore them all so that I don't encourage the sender. Also I don't know where I'd put fifty pounds of lobster.

And the subject lines are so intriguing, like the one I got from the Department of Violations which says, "Regarding your speeding ticket." That got my attention and I haven't even gotten a speeding ticket—lately.

I got an email today telling me I could make money while I sleep. Coincidentally I got another message telling me I could lose weight while I sleep. That would make my nights more productive than my days, especially since I spend so much of my days going through email.

I've been spammed, scammed and damned so many times online that I'm most tempted by the new breed of spam I've been receiving lately. It comes with catchy subject lines like "Tired of these emails?" "Killing spam for fun and profit" and

"WARNING: Internet Reached Max Capacity."
Gee, how could that happen?

I'm getting dozens of messages a day warning me my CVS Card Rewards are expiring (I don't have a CVS card). Offering to help cure my tinnitus (I don't have tinnitus either). Telling me about singles in my neighborhood and without even knowing what neighborhood I live in. It's uncanny!

The spammers are wasting my time, increasing my chances of missing a legitimate message and tarnishing the good name of a perfectly fine meat product. I've had it! So I got myself a new email address, set the spam filter on high and started hitting the "block sender" option every time I get a junk email to the old address. Then I do a little trash talk: "Take that, you cyber scum!"

I don't think they can hear me though. Plus I'm getting a repetitive motion injury in my right wrist. Still it gives me some small satisfaction, at least until I accidentally block a legitimate email. Forgive me if you emailed me recently and haven't heard back.

One day I took my frustration out on a phone solicitor who made the mistake of calling while I was knee deep in e-poo. She informed me that her company was detecting a large amount of junk on my computer, and if I gave her my bank account information, she would be happy to help me get rid of it. I told her I was detecting large amounts of junk on my phone too, then I accused her of being nothing but Track R Bravo with a telephone.

I never get that grumpy at people—unless I'm related to them. I felt bad the minute I hung up. She has to make a living too. Maybe I should have been more encouraging. Next time I'll say, "You have many strong points, not the least of which is persistence. You could do something useful—and honest—with your life. And by the way, what's your email address? I'd like to share it with my friend Dura Bowl."

Mad as they make me, I believe spammers have a lot to teach us about effective marketing. Really. Don't let the fact that they can't spell fool you. Clearly spam is the smart way to go if you want to sell a product, market a service or acquire other people's credit card numbers. Between deleting messages I've picked up the following clever strategies to help you do it:

1. First you must choose a pseudonym. This is important. If your product is like many others sold with spam, you may not want your parents to know you're selling it.

There are three approaches you can use when choosing your alias. First you could try an unusual name. People can't help but be drawn to those with exotic-sounding names like I. M. Floating, Opulence Here's How or Nicoteenia Caffeinia,

A common name like David Smith or Jill Jones can also be effective because the recipient can't help but wonder, "Wasn't she in my fifth-grade class?" Or, "Did I meet him at my niece's wedding?" Obviously if people think they know you, they're more likely to give you their credit card number.

Finally, you could choose an organizational-sounding name. I can't resist Prize Notification Department and Internet Regulator no matter how many times I see them—or how they're spelled.

2. You'll need to create attention-grabbing subject lines. Here are some creative examples that worked on me: "People say you're really smart," "World's coolest mini stunt car" and "Want to own your own spaceship?" How could I not open the message with the clever subject line, "I think you'll like this as much as I think you will."

But be careful you don't promise too much in your subject line. "Be wealthy beyond your wildest dreams" might leave your readers disappointed with your content since you have no way of knowing how wild their dreams actually are. And also try to avoid turning your recipients off. "Thicker hair in 30 seconds" is frightening even to the hairless.

3. Flatter your recipient. I never get tired of seeing "You deserve to be rich," "Your life experience alone is worth a Ph.D.," and "You would look even more ravishing in a new Swiss replica watch!"

4. Don't fret about the mechanics of your writing. You can draw attention away from spelling and grammar errors by using plenty of CAPLITAL LETERS AND EXCAVATION PONTS!!!!!!!!!! See what I mean?

5. Forget everything you've ever heard about target marketing. Spread your message like dandelion seeds in the wind. Just type "CONFIDEN-TIAL" or "You've been selected from 30 million people" at the top of your message and all the recipients will believe they're the only one you've contacted—even the women receiving your barbershop perfect sideburns message.

6. Finally and most importantly, don't give up. Be relentless. Be prolific. Be a pain.

There you have it: the six magical rules used by effective spammers. Trust me; these really work.

They must. They KEEP!!!!ON!!!!DOING IT!!!!!!

Seriously though, I'm always tempted to write back and give spammers a piece of what's left of my mind. "Are you dumber than lint? What are you thinking? We can send information faster than at any other time in history, and what do you send: 'New Royal Family Secret,' 'Belly Fat Be Gone!' and 'Male Enhancement Solution'."

But I believe there's always hope for rehabilitation so I've composed the following kinder, gentler message, though I have yet to send it:

Dear Spammer,

Your offer is…uh…fascinating. Unfortunately, at this point I'm not the least bit interested. What's more, I'm quite sure I never will be, but thank you so much anyway.

May I suggest a career change? You clearly have many fine qualities—persistence and perseverance, to name a few of the more obvious ones. You can type—sort of. You've got guts; most people would be too embarrassed to say the things you say. And you show amazing creativity in the way you continue to come up with new ways to say the same thing: "Give me your money."

Have you ever considered using your many gifts to make a positive contribution, by which I mean get a real job?

A bit of advice though: If you want to be successful in your new career, you may want to invest in a good grammar book and learn to use your spellchecker. Forgive me for being so particular, but I couldn't help but question your credibility when you tried to sell doctoral diplomas with an email that said, "Get a Dekgree. No books, no clasjeses." Of course I do realize they don't cover spelling in doctoral programs.

By the way, congratulations on your dekgree, but if I were you I wouldn't mention it on any job applications. You may also want to consider changing your name before you head out into the job market. Trust is the foundation of all good business relationships, and some people find it hard to trust someone with a name like UR Gullible or Falsehood AlMega. If that's your given name, forgive me—and your parents. It's easy to understand why you turned out the way you did, self-fulfilling prophesies being what they are. You have my sympathy—but not my credit card number.

Finally, in your next career try not to be—how

can I say this nicely—so annoying. There are just certain things no one wants to know about your personal life. And even your mother doesn't want to hear from you as often as I do. Follow my advice and you could still make her proud one day. But please don't feel like you need to email me your thanks.

P.S. You of all people should understand why I felt the need to hit send ten thousand times.

Reader, you may wonder why I'm in such a dither about a little spam in my inbox. It's simple. I'm afraid my ship is going to come in some day and I won't be at the dock to meet it because of a bunch of scammers. I've worried about this ever since I read the story of Australian writer Helen Garner. Apparently she got a message in her junk email folder telling her she'd won a prestigious writing prize, but the sender needed her phone number to discuss it with her. What would you do? Go meet the ship? Email them right back? Not me. I would have deleted the message faster than you can say, "That's no ship. That's a garbage scow."

Ms. Garner responded, but only after doing some research. And it's a good thing she did because that's how she learned she'd won one of the 2016 Windham-Campbell writing prizes worth $150,000. After reading about Helen Garner, I went directly to my spam folder to see if I might have a ship floating around in mine too. And if not a ship, at least a little skiff or an old fishing boat.

The spam folder for my newer account had just twenty-five spam messages in it. None of them looked like a ship coming in, though there was an advertisement for private yacht rentals—all sizes and budgets available. Incidentally, there was also a really good deal on bowling shoes.

The spam folder for my older account contained 2,032 spam messages dating back a month. Holy inbox! That's an average of sixty-seven spam messages a day. If I had to read all those every day, I'd never get through my legitimate emails. Oh, wait. I don't.

I didn't take the time to read all 2,032 spam messages either. But before I emptied the folder, I scanned through the advertisements for DUI lawyers, cat food coupons and lonely singles in my neighborhood. As far as I could tell, there were no ships, just a whole lot of dinghies.

It's just as well. If I had found an email promising

large amounts of cash, I wouldn't have believed it anyway. You get a little cynical after you've deleted a few hundred messages offering easy hair removal and large loans without credit checks.

No, if anyone wants to alert me that I've won a $150,000 prize they're going to need another way to do it. And it won't be by phone either. I don't answer unless I recognize the number, thanks to the epidemic of robocalls and helpful people wanting to fix my computer that's not broken.

They can't just come knocking either. I stopped opening my front door to people I don't know after I was scammed by a magazine sales person claiming to be raising money for college. I don't know if he ever went to college, but I know I never got my magazine.

If my ship comes in by mail, it's likely to get buried by credit card offers and insurance offers from the AARP. By the time I get to it, they'll have given my prize to someone else.

So yes, I'm concerned that someday my ship will come in and I won't be at the dock to meet it. And if it shows up at my front door or by snail mail, telephone or email, the chances are good I'll sink it myself before it gets to shore.

Shredding Your Way
to Happiness

I have a highly efficient filing system for my family's mail and other important documents. It's on my kitchen counter—just inches from the toaster and the sugar canister. Every bit of junk mail, every greeting card, every letter from an insurance company, every single piece of paper that comes to our home goes there. I'm proud to say that I've never toasted an important document, but I have buttered a few.

When I clean the kitchen, which I sometimes do, I sort through the pile, throw some pieces away and handle others in an appropriate and business-like manner: I put them into other piles. The bills go in the to-be-paid pile and the papers we should save go in the to-be-filed pile.

Then I run out of time and push the remaining pieces back into a heap; they'll be there the next time I clean. Meanwhile I start, that very day, putting new paper on top of the heap. There are drawbacks to my system, the major one being that some of the things on the bottom of the stack are now five years old.

When I do go through the stack, naturally I find some items that should be destroyed in order to protect my identity, such as it is. In the old days, I tore them up by hand. Then I put half the pieces in the bathroom trash and half the pieces in the kitchen trash where egg shells and leftover tomato soup would render those that weren't already buttered equally unrecognizable. Any self-respecting identity thief would really have to want my identity to steal my identity. And speaking from experience, I'm not sure it would be worth it for them. It's not that great being me.

Obviously this process took a lot of work, so I tended to put if off. But my life changed dramatically the day I was inspired to clean the closet in my guest bedroom. I didn't do it, but I was inspired. And I did remove four giant boxes of checks probably dating back to the first checking account I had in eighth grade. As you can imagine, destroying all those checks with my old method would have taken a lot of time and a lot of leftover tomato soup.

Instead I bought a shredder. What an invention! I had no idea how relaxing using a shredder could be—as long as you keep your fingers out of it. And as you sit before the shredder disposing of old checks, receipts and junk mail, you can't help but examine your life. I was shocked to see how much I eat out but I was thrilled to learn that, based on all the credit card applications I receive, I must be an excellent credit risk.

Mostly though I began to see shredding as a defense against the onslaught of paper pouring into my home. I'm sure I heard once that technology would decrease paperwork. Turns out it just allowed us to generate more of it more quickly. We no longer have paper trails; we have paper freeways. And a large part of my paper freeway is paved with junk mail.

It is true that I get less mail than I once did and it is also true that I toss more of it without adding it to the stack on my kitchen counter than I once did.

I'm no longer taken in by the fact that every other piece of junk mail says ATTENTION: IMPORTANT INFORMATION INSIDE or DO NOT DISCARD, which is the direct mail equivalent of crying wolf. I'm afraid someday I'll miss a jury summons or a letter from the IRS because it says IMPORTANT DOCUMENTS ENCLOSED.

Still I can't keep up with my mail. I read once that if you're an average American—and how many of us can claim that—you'll spend eight months of your life sifting through junk mail.

A typical week's mail at the Rosby home contains an average of ten advertising flyers, nine credit card applications, eight bills, seven solicitations for donations to worthy causes, six solicitations for donations to unworthy causes, five political fundraising letters, four magazines, three invitations to switch our television service, two packets of coupons and a partridge in a pear tree. I'm exaggerating. There's no partridge though we do regularly hear from a few dodo birds.

You'll notice I didn't mention letters on my list. That's because I seldom get letters. Careful mathematical calculation shows that if ceasing to open junk mail would save eight months of my life, not opening first class letters would save me about thirteen and a half minutes. If that sounds low, it's because most of the people who write me are not first class. I'm kidding!

I just don't receive letters anymore. I used to. Walking downtown to the post office was the highlight of my summer days when I was a child. I had at least a dozen pen pals and I answered their letters immediately. I even kept a rough draft of every letter I wrote so that I would never tell them the same news twice. Considering the highlight of my day was walking downtown to get the mail, you can see how that could happen.

But it wasn't only letters I was waiting for. At that point I thought any mail was good mail, so I regularly sent for catalogs and free samples of chewing gum and cosmetics. Even so, I didn't get mail every day, even every week. And my walk to the post office often ended in disappointment.

When I was in college, getting the mail was more rewarding. Not only did I receive letters, I also occasionally received the college student's dream mail, the care package filled with all the crushed cookies I could eat.

After college my third class mail quickly caught

up to my first class mail. I still looked forward to getting the mail though, because I still got real letters, probably because I still wrote real letters. But alas, where once upon a time I wrote every letter twice, eventually I stopped writing them even once, and apparently so did everyone else.

Today I get an occasional envelope that looks like it might be an actual letter. On closer inspection I find it only looks that way because of the computer-generated handwriting. In my opinion this is the height of deception and manipulation. And it works every time.

But as I've already established, that doesn't mean I don't get mail. Boy do I get mail. I have to wonder: how did I get on every mailing list in the free world? Even more remarkable, how do they know so much about me? A look at my mail presents an amazingly accurate portrait of who I am. The other day I received a brochure from a company offering to clean my furnace and ducts. In bold letters at the top was the declaration, "You should not have to dust your home every two days!" I have always felt that way, which is why I don't.

On the same day, I received a flyer telling me I spend too much money on car insurance and one promoting a fabulous new pill guaranteed to help reduce my belly fat. How did they know?

And you may not believe this, but a surprising number of people who don't even know me are willing to loan me money. This is amazing to me since most people who do know me wouldn't loan me a dime.

Every other day I receive at least one credit card application or letter from a bank inviting me to, as one put it, "exercise my financial freedom" by borrowing money. While financial freedom sounds terribly exciting to me, somehow the more debt I have the less financially free I feel. Buying on credit means making payments on something after I've already sold it at a garage sale.

Still I'm tempted after the avalanche of stunningly beautiful and very persuasive mail pieces I've received lately. They flatter me. "You're the kind of person who knows where you're going!" (Into debt?) "A credit line up to $10,000…because you are responsible and being responsible has its rewards." (How responsible would I be if I ran up a $10,000 credit card debt?) "We're offering you the smart rate for smart people." (I'm smart enough to see the smart rate only lasts three months.)

They appeal to my dreams. "Travel to an exotic spot. Enjoy the finer things. Whatever your dreams, this card gives you the power to make them reality." (Except my dream of being debt free.)

One company tempts me with a card decorated with mountains. "The peaks, the plains, the tranquility and now the card. If you love the natural beauty of our majestic mountains (I do), you'll want to get the new no-annual fee card." (I will?)

And they play on my anxiety about money. "How can we make your life easier?" (Give me the cash and don't ask me to pay it back!)

Thank goodness for my shredder. I only wish I'd gotten it sooner—maybe my counter would be cleaner. Of course the shredder has its drawbacks. It doesn't give a warning: "IRS code requires that you keep this document for at least seven years." Or "STOP! That's your electric bill!" And documents cannot be put back together once they've been shredded—which I suppose is the point of having a shredder.

Clearing paper jams is intimidating. The shredder grinds to a halt and I can't help but think of every snow blower and table saw mishap I've ever heard about.

And I worry about the effect butter, sugar and toast crumbs will have on it. I'll shut it down if my office ever starts smelling like breakfast.

Sound-Off on Online Shopping

I type in my name, address, credit card number, discount code, my mother's maiden name, my first pet's name, the name of my best friend in fourth grade, the model of my first car and the nickname of my second grade teacher's oldest child and...ta-dah!

The online form locks up. I close out, go back in and do the whole thing once more and...it locks up again.

I have two choices: I can give up, or I can call the business in whatever faraway place it is, wait on hold while a recording says over and over, "Thank you for your patience," and I scream, "What patience," until I'm finally able to talk to a real person who may or may not want to talk to me.

This is a true story—mostly—and it illustrates one of the reasons I'd rather shop locally than let my fingers do the walking with online shopping. Here are a few more.

1.   When you shop locally, knowledgeable store associates can not only help you choose the right product for your needs, they can also tell you how the darn thing works. I assume you already know how to use dog treats and dishtowels, but you might need some coaching on a laptop or a chainsaw. A little advice could mean the difference between many years of using the product happily or tossing it at the wall when you can't get it to work the way you think it should which, by the way, could void your warranty.

And don't you love how clothing store employees come to your dressing room door to offer you another size when you've been a bit too optimistic? And how they reassure you when you're standing in front of a three-way mirror eyeing yourself critically in a stylish cocktail dress—and knee socks.

Oh sure, when you're posed in front of your bedroom mirror checking out an outfit you purchased online, your children might wander in and offer an opinion. "Nice. What's for dinner?" But that's not the same.

2. It's good to try before you buy, except for groceries. Don't do that. Honestly some of us don't even know what size we wear. Most women I know have a range of sizes in their closets and not just because they've been a range of sizes. We all know sizing varies based on the cost of the clothing— maybe the more money we have, the more delusional we become.

But even if sizing were consistent, women's figures are not. Two women wearing the same dress in the same size won't fill it out the same. And neither of them will fill it out the way the model on the tag does.

3. Before you buy something locally, you can smell it, touch it and shake it, though if you shake it too hard, you may have to buy it even if you don't like the way it smells.

When you order online there's no guarantee that what you see on the screen is what you'll get in the mail. Do an internet search of online shopping scams and you can see a stylish jumpsuit that looked more like pink surgical scrubs when the buyer received it, a bridesmaid dress that bore a striking resemblance to a night gown I once owned and an attractive three-piece bedding set that was only one pillowcase when it arrived—and not an attractive one.

4. All of the above means you're less likely to have to return your purchase. And returning products is the worst part of shopping, mainly because nothing ever fits back in the box you bought it in. It's as though new purchases expand when they're exposed to oxygen.

Some companies offer free shipping. Big deal. If they made returns easier, they'd really have something to brag about. And by "easier" I mean they'd send a friendly representative to your house to package the item, take it to the post office and stand in line to mail it for you. Maybe they'd even pick up a roll of stamps for you while they're there.

5. When you shop locally, you can shop with friends and make it a social occasion. Sitting on the couch with a group of pals all pointing at their iPhones isn't an occasion; it's just another day.

6. You can hide purchases when you buy them locally. If you buy something you don't want your

husband to know about, maybe something for his birthday—or something for your birthday—you can keep it in the car until he's not home. If you buy it online, you have to make sure you're home the day it arrives and you have to have a good story ready for when he says, "Was that UPS at the door?"

7.   Shopping locally burns more calories than sitting at your computer with a bowl of maple nut. Not only are you racking up a lot of steps on the old Fitbit walking from store to store, you're hauling your purchases like a pack horse. You'll probably come out ahead even if you stop for a donut and a Frappuccino while you're out.

8.   Shopping locally is good for the community. When my son was young, I spent many hours watching Little League baseball games and I never once saw the name Amazon, Wayfair or Overstock. com emblazoned on the back of a uniform. Doing business with the good people who are regularly hit up for all manner of donations and sponsorships seems like the least we can do.

Having said all of that, I will admit there are times when shopping online is the way to go. Maybe the product you need isn't available locally, or maybe you're quarantined or under house arrest. Maybe you're embarrassed to be seen buying a particular product, like head lice shampoo or a copy of *Fifty Shades of Grey*. Or maybe you're not the type to worry about internet security, and you're a whiz at filling out online forms—in which case I could really use some help.

May I Speak to a
Real Person, Please?

I once ordered antivirus software from a particular company. As it turned out, it would have been easier and more pleasant to have a virus.

I was unable to download the software—not surprisingly—so as directed, I emailed the support desk for help. Then several days later I emailed again. When no help was forthcoming, I purchased another brand and emailed the first company asking for a refund.

Then they finally offered to help. Then they

couldn't find any record of my order. Then they asked me to tell them what happened. Then they asked me to tell them again.

After more than a month and a dozen emails back and forth, they sent me a message saying, "Unfortunately, these issues are best resolved over the phone. Please call at your convenience."

They must have meant at their convenience because they didn't include a toll-free number and they left me on hold for twenty minutes—twice. Eventually I was able to speak to an actual human, or so I thought. I'll call him SJ for "Smug Jerk"—because he was one, not because it's his name. I forgot that, but his mother probably even calls him Smug Jerk.

Anyway, his helpful response was, "You're past the thirty-day refund period."

"But I've been emailing your company for thirty days."

"Doesn't matter. That's our policy."

Customer service rule number one: Never say, "That's our policy." Even if it is. The only thing more infuriating to a customer is spitting on them. SJ probably would have done that too if he weren't far away, hiding in his little cubicle in the bowels of some giant tech firm.

SJ said his supervisor would email me the next day. I told him I'd rather give him my phone number.

"He won't call."

"Why not? Your email said these issues are best resolved by phone."

"Only within thirty days."

That's when I did something that I normally reserve only for the people I love and care about the most: I yelled at SJ. I told him his customer service skills stink. His company stinks and his cubicle probably stinks too. Actually I don't remember what I said, but I know it did nothing to change his company's policy.

And he was right. His supervisor didn't call. Nor did he email. And I'm still waiting for my refund.

Customer service has changed in the age of online shopping. Now we spend our days emailing faceless companies, being put on hold by people who may or may not go to lunch while we wait, live chatting on our computer with technicians who can type faster than we can and talking to recordings, my personal favorite.

They're not all bad. Not long ago I called a particular company to cancel three magazine subscriptions. And the nice lady who answered the phone didn't even try to talk me out of it. That's because she was a recording. A very nice recording. I'll call her Digital Dora though she didn't actually introduce herself.

She asked me to say the name of each magazine and after each one she said pleasantly, "I'm sorry you didn't enjoy the magazine." Three times, she said that. But she didn't sound sorry, so I didn't feel bad canceling like I would have if Digital Dora had been a real human being working on commission.

A conversation I had with another recording took twice as long and was a lot less productive. I'd already kicked the wall and cursed the credit card company by the time I got around to calling the customer service number on the back of my credit card. What I wanted at that moment was a helpful reassuring human being, or a reasonable facsimile—like Digital Dora. Instead I got Recorded Rita. "If you would like help in English, please say 'English' or press one."

"English or press one."

"I'm sorry. I didn't hear you. If you would like help in English, please say 'English' or press one."

Apparently she didn't get the joke. I said "English."

"Please say 'lost card protection,' 'new card features,' 'rate quotes' or 'problems with my bill.'"

"Huh?"

"I'm sorry, I didn't hear you. Please say 'lost card protection,' 'new card features,' 'rate quotes' or 'problems with my bill.'"

"I don't understand my stupid bill." I'm not what you'd call a quick learner.

"I'm sorry, I didn't hear you. Please say 'lost card protection,' 'new card features'…."

"Problems with my bill." She'd beaten me into submission.

"Are you having problems with your bill? Please say 'yes' or 'no.'"

"Well duh!"

"I'm sorry. I didn't hear you. Are you having problems with your bill? Please say…."

"Yes," I screamed. Then I remembered this call might be monitored for quality assurance purposes.

"I'm sorry to hear that." But she didn't sound sorry at all. "I'll transfer you to our billing department."

"Wait! Are there any real people there?"

She didn't answer. Clearly Rita lacks empathy, she has poor hearing and she has no sense of humor.

But I'll say this for her. She never loses her temper and she's very polite. Her last words to me were, "Thank you for using your (name of worthless) credit card."

"I'm sorry," I said. "I didn't hear you."

Vexation and Obfuscation in Communication

When I picked up my mail today, I was thrilled to find not only the fascinating notice of amendments to my credit card agreement, but also a spell-binding semi-annual report from one of the companies represented in my retirement account. I would have loved to sit down and read them both right then. But there was dinner to make and dishes to do, and with one thing and another it wasn't until after 8 o'clock that I finally cozied up on the couch to enjoy some me time and a little light reading.

I lie.

If I'm ever trapped on a desert island with nothing to read but mail from insurance and financial companies, I'll give up reading forever and spend the rest of my days reciting all the Dr. Seuss I remember until I get rescued or die waiting.

For one thing, even if I remembered to bring my reading glasses to the island, which is unlikely, I probably wouldn't have any more luck locating them there than I do in my house. And you do need reading glasses to read much of what we receive from insurance and financial companies. Their employees must have better eyes than the rest of us.

But the bigger issue is that when I do locate my reading glasses and wade through a paragraph or two, I have no idea what I just read. You may not be aware of this, but as a writer, I attempt to make everything I write clear, even the outright lies.

It's obvious to me there are writers out there who don't give a flying semi-colon about making their work understandable, and many of them work in industries that hold our financial lives in their hands. Don't they know that most of their customers don't have law degrees?

Maybe I'm just slow, but when I take the time to

read the privacy policy from a credit card company and it discusses "sharing non-public personal public information," I think being understood is the last thing on the writer's mind.

When I read, "Coverage is not provided for your policy or any portion of it that is not guaranteed by the insurer or for which you have assumed the risk, such as a variable contract sold by prospectus," I don't feel like that writer is trying to connect with the reader.

And when I read "Contract owners' payments will be allocated by the company separate account to procure shares of the Fund chosen by the contract owner, and are subject to any limits or conditions set forth in the agreement," I start to question the value of my college degree. And I do have one.

I paid good money to get majors in both journalism and communication and a minor in English, and I can't read my own mail. Maybe if I'd taken enough classes to make that English minor a major, everything would be clear. As it is my best translation of any financial document I get in the mail is, "Oh! Is that you, customer? We didn't really think anyone would read this far." And that's probably a safe bet.

But why? Are they showing off? "I know a

closed-end fund from a unit investment trust and you don't. Too bad, so sad for you!"

Are they passive-aggressive? "Yes, we're required to send you this but there's no law that says we have to make it readable."

Or are they purposely trying to hide their meaning, even mislead us? How can anyone who writes, "Notwithstanding anything to the contrary contained in this agreement, any subsequent execution of the elective deferral options will be based on established measures," really have my best interests at heart?

And what's the impact on us? You may not realize this, but incomprehensible medical bills and complicated insurance documents are the main reasons many a poor soul comes successfully through a serious illness and the ensuing treatments and then goes ahead and dies anyway.

I recall the day my husband and I signed the papers to finance my home. It took us twenty minutes to sign a stack of papers that would have taken three months to read and a lifetime to comprehend. But we didn't have three months to read them so the loan officer smiled sweetly as she handed us page after page, explaining in simple terms what each of them said. If she could explain the documents that simply, why couldn't the writer make them that simple? Or was the loan officer lying? Will she call us one day to tell us she's moving into our house and converting our guest room into servant's quarters—for us? When I protest will she say, "But you signed the papers"?

I don't know about you, but I've never read a prospectus cover to cover—though I have read a prospectus cover. Who knows what I'm missing? Maybe I have even less money than I think I do.

If you have read a prospectus cover to cover, I know some things about you without ever having met you: You're smarter and more patient than I am. You have more time on your hands than I do. And you not only have reading glasses, you can find them.

When I do attempt to read one, I get stuck on phrases like: "Risks include, but are not limited to delivery failure, default by the other party, or the lack of ability or opportunity to close out a position because the trading market becomes, or is likely to become, illiquid." Oh.

After years of wading through all the documents it takes to be a semi-responsible adult, I've discovered the writers' devious methods, if not their meaning.

First, they never use one word when a whole phrase will do. They don't say "because," they say "due to the fact that…" They don't just "estimate," they "make an approximation as to how many." They don't just receive your letter, they "acknowledge receipt of your recent correspondence." Before you know it, a paragraph's worth of information fills twelve pages—twelve very dull pages.

Second, they never use a common word when they can use an obscure one. They don't "prove," they "substantiate." They don't "learn," they "ascertain." They don't "substitute," they "subrogate," leaving you to wonder what just happened.

They save the plain English for information you already know. "You are responsible for this bill." "The post office will not deliver without a stamp." If they think we're that dim-witted, you know they don't really expect us to understand when they say, "Our share is that proportion of the loss that the applicable maximum value under this policy bears to the total amount of insurance covering the loss at the time that it is incurred."

Then our basement floods and they're glad we didn't understand.

Decision Time in
Aisle One

I'm putting off getting my produce, dairy products and frozen foods until I've loaded everything else into my grocery cart. Otherwise my milk will curdle, my ice cream will melt and my perishables will perish while I stand here trying to decide between whole wheat, crushed wheat, honey wheat, honey bran, sunflower, hazel nut, twelve grain, organic and classic bread.

Shopping for groceries—or anything else for that matter—is challenging for the indecisive. I finally choose twelve grain, and head to the most difficult department of all: Personal Care.

Before me lies a display of toothpaste as far as the eye can see. I prefer gel to paste and mint to cinnamon, but do I want mouthwash, peroxide or baking soda in my toothpaste? And what do I need more? Enamel care, tarter control, cavity protection, sensitive teeth, whitening, extra whitening or breath freshening? Don't answer that. I choose cavity protection. I don't have time to go to the dentist, not when I spend so much time at the grocery store.

I'm exhausted. And I still need shampoo. Do I want salon formula, color-safe, volume-enhancing, anti-residue or moisture therapy? Yes. But I can't get it all in one bottle, so I settle for moisture therapy because therapy might be just what I need after choosing toothpaste and shampoo.

Then I take a deep breath and prepare to spend the rest of the afternoon in the hand lotion aisle because that's how long it's going to take me to decide if I want lotion that evens skin tone and improves texture; firms skin and gives it radiance; hydrates hands and strengthens nails or protects hands from the sun and won't wash off in water.

I'm paralyzed by so many choices. Fortunately, I

have some coping mechanisms. Unfortunately, none of them work.

1. I put off grocery shopping until all that's left to eat in our home is baking soda and condiments. You might think this is counterproductive since I'll just have more to shop for when I finally do get to the store. And you'd be right.

2. I pick a favorite and stick with it, no matter how many new options are presented. For example, I always choose the same brand of vanilla yogurt. Boring? Maybe. But have you seen the yogurt aisle lately? At my favorite ice cream place, I have a turtle sundae every time. Don't judge. It's delicious and you'll appreciate it if you're ever in line behind me.

3. When I can't decide between two items, I buy both. I have two sweaters that look exactly alike, except one is purple and one is blue. And I have another set of duplicate sweaters, one blue and one pink, for the same reason. My closet looks like I live with an identical twin. Obviously this doesn't work when I'm faced with larger decisions, like when we're choosing paint for our house—or buying a new one. But it does work when I'm buying cookies.

4. I choose the one that's cheapest, but not because I'm thrifty. No one who buys their sweaters

two at a time could be called thrifty. It's just that when I can't decide between aromatherapy, oxygenated cleansing action, degreasing or gentle-on-hands dish soap, I have to base my decision on something, and basing it solely on the way it smells doesn't seem appropriate.

5. Faced with too many decisions, I choose... nothing. I'm not alone. In one study of the so-called paradox of choice, two psychologists found that customers presented with six varieties of jam were more likely to buy one than those who were offered twenty-four varieties. They were more likely to run screaming from the store.

My grocery store has at least that many varieties of jam which is why I use cinnamon on my toast. The only decision is how much sugar to add.

I've now made it to laundry soap. Do I want liquid or powder? Do I prefer mountain fresh, mountain spring, springtime or fragrance free? Do I need detergent with bleach, without bleach or with bleach alternative? Do I need my detergent to dissolve quickly, deep clean or fight odors? And if I choose deep cleaning, will my detergent dissolve too slowly and my laundry smell bad?

I believe we each have the ability to make a

limited number of choices every day. And I worry that if we use up our allotment on frivolous decisions like mint or wintergreen, liquid or powder, we won't have any left for the bigger issues that arise: Term or whole life? Rent or own? Dine in or carryout? That's why I avoid making any major decisions for a day or two after buying groceries, and I recommend you do the same. But you decide—if you can.

I've been at the grocery store nearly an hour now, and with the exception of a loaf of bread, I still don't have any food. Man cannot live on bread alone. Neither can woman, even if it is twelve grain.

I pick up my pace. I hurry past the baking aisle; I don't bake. I skip the dog food; I don't have a dog. I dash past baby food; I don't have a baby either.

I'm undeterred by the many peanut butter choices—creamy, crunchy, extra crunchy, natural, low fat or low carb. I don't need peanut butter.

I stand confidently in front of the canned veggies. I like beets but not pickled beets. And I like my canned tomatoes diced so I don't have to do it myself.

But then…I round the corner at the canned soups. There's a cream of something soup for every day of the year and almost that many pasta choices:

rotelle, cavatelli, farfalle, fusilli, mostaccioli, penne, rigatoni, ziti. Huh?

And Mother Nature can't be beat for variety. I need lettuce, but do I want romaine, red leaf, Bibb, or iceberg? I want apples—I'm just not sure if I want Gala, Fuji, McIntosh, Golden Delicious, Red Delicious, Honeycrisp or Granny Smith. I haven't been this overwhelmed since hand lotion.

At last, weary and confused, I head back to the dairy aisle for milk (skim, one percent, two percent, whole, lactose free, chocolate, almond, cashew or soy), butter (salted, unsalted, low fat or regular) and cheese (too many to mention).

I have now spent more time choosing my groceries than I spent choosing my car, but I'm finally done for another week. I might even be home in time for dinner, though it's probably too late to cook it.

By the time I get to the checkout line, my defenses are worn down like a dieter's resistance in a donut shop. The only thing that keeps me from grabbing a handful of candy bars in the checkout aisle is that I can't decide which ones I want.

Wait a minute. I forgot one thing. God help me! I need a birthday card.

Tired of Surveys?
1) Yes 2) No 3) Maybe

This may come as a surprise to you, but a lot of people care about my opinion and some of them are even willing to pay for it, or at least give me a coupon for it. Lucky for them I always have an opinion—plus I'm almost always right.

That must be why, in the last few weeks alone, I've been surveyed by two clothing stores, a hotel, an office supply store, three restaurants, a bank, a pet store, a political group and the flashlight app on my cell phone.

Clearly I'm a much sought-after thought leader. Maybe you are too. That's why I'm inviting you to fill out the following survey:

The Survey about Surveys

1. How many surveys have you been invited to fill out in the last month?

   ❏ None. Nobody cares what I think.

   ❏ Just a few, but I was (circle all that apply) out of the country/under quarantine/in a coma.

   ❏ If surveys were dollar bills, I could afford health insurance.

2. How many surveys have you actually completed in the last month?

   ❏ None. I told you; nobody cares what I think.

   ❏ Just a few. I only fill out surveys from (circle all that apply) organizations I love/organizations I work for/organizations I'm mad at but afraid to say what I think to their face.

❏ I've lost count but it must be a lot because I have a stack of coupons the size of a garden shed.

3. When you fill out a survey, how do you feel about sharing your contact information?

❏ I share my name and contact information in case I can be of further assistance. (Also so they know where to send my cash prize when I win it.)

❏ I prefer to remain anonymous because I'm afraid (circle all that apply) they won't like what I have to say/they'll like what I have to say so much they'll add me to their email list.

4. When you answer a survey, what is your motivation?

❑ Impact. I love that I can help change the world by sharing my deepest thoughts with people who really listen.

❑ Financial. Coupons and the possibility of winning cash are part of my retirement strategy.

❑ Guilt. They need me. If I don't answer the survey and they go out of business, it will be my fault.

❑ What motivation? If I were motivated I'd be doing my dishes instead of filling out this survey.

5. What is the best incentive you've ever received for answering a survey?

❑ The satisfaction of knowing I've helped an organization improve their customer service.

❏ $5000!

❏ A coupon for free French fries.

6. How do you prefer to be surveyed?

❏ By mail so that I can do the survey at my leisure…or never.

❏ By email so that I can do the survey at my leisure…or never

❏ By phone so that I can take a break from dinner with my family to answer it.

7. In your opinion, are surveys effective?

❏ Yes.

❏ No.

❏ Effective at what?

8.   What is your overall satisfaction level with surveys?

❏ I love them! I just quit my day job so I can fill out surveys full-time.

❏ I can take them or leave them. Mostly I leave them.

❏ Make it stop. Please make it stop.

CHAPTER FOUR

Where Are Your Manners?

Where Are Your Manners?

I've always dreamed of being an etiquette columnist. Readers could write me with their questions and I could answer them in the pages of newspapers across the country. I'd be the next Miss Manners. I've always liked telling people what to do.

Unfortunately no one ever asks me etiquette questions. I'm not going to let that stand in the way of my dream and your enlightenment though. I'm going to share my top eight rules of etiquette even though you didn't ask for them.

1. Don't give unsolicited advice.

I can but you shouldn't.

2. Don't overshare.

I've been on the receiving end of oversharing many times. Probably on the oversharing end too, but we won't talk about that now. Two of the most frequently overshared topics these days seem to be food allergies and food preferences. For example, another guest at a potluck I attended recently asked me which dish was mine. I told her I brought my bok choy salad which, by the way, is fabulous. She made a face like she'd just eaten spoiled sushi and said, "Ewww. I don't like bok choy at all." I didn't need to know that.

Many a restaurant employee has been embarrassed by a customer's description of what gluten or dairy does to her digestive system. The wait staff doesn't need to know you're lactose intolerant; just don't order the cheese soup.

3. Don't say everything you think.

Whenever I'm tempted to share something negative, hurtful or gossipy about someone else I ask myself how they'd feel if they walked in at that moment. If the answer is hurt, betrayed or mad enough to give me a good thrashing, I keep it to myself. I'm just that kind of person. Plus, more than once I have gossiped about someone, and they have walked in at that moment.

4. Always return phone calls.

At least always return my phone calls. When someone doesn't return my call, I assume I'm not important enough for them—or that they're dead. Is that something you really want getting out?

5. Avoid telling medical horror stories to sick people.

You mention an unfortunate condition or pending medical procedure to some people and they launch into a detailed account of their own similar experience. They'll recall all the details with relish and tell you how dreadfully awful and horribly painful it was, how they nearly died and how there were many times they wished they'd just gone ahead and done it. When I've encountered this sort of response, it was all I could do not to say, "Thank you for squashing all my remaining hope. Will you be at the funeral?"

6. Never say, "I told you so" when someone is to blame for their problems.

Believe me, they've already learned their lesson. Plus they might punch you. Then you'll learn a lesson too. I promise not to say I told you so.

7.   Make introductions whenever you're with two or more people who don't know each other. If, however, you cannot remember one or both of their names, you have two choices. You can pretend they already know each other or you can flee the scene.

I'm joking. But remembering names is such a problem for so many people that I have included tips in the next essay which I published previously to wide acclaim. Actually there was no acclaim whatsoever. Rule Number 7½: You shouldn't lie and neither should an etiquette columnist.

8.   Before you ask a deeply personal question, consider the very real possibility that it may be none of your business.

I know; just because it's none of your concern doesn't mean you don't want to know.

It's not my place as an aspiring etiquette columnist to suggest you make a spit-in-their-eye sarcastic response if you're on the receiving end of such a question. It may even go against the Etiquette Columnist Code of Ethics to suggest it. But I just can't help myself.

I've noticed that we are most tempted to ask

personal questions of those standing on the brink of life's major transitions. For example, the moment a couple starts dating, those who know them—and even those who don't know them—begin asking, "When are you getting married?" My suggested response is, "We are married—just not to each other."

When the couple does marry, their family and friends begin to ask, "When are you going to have a baby?" One appropriate response is, "There are just so few people we can trust to babysit."

When the couple eventually does have a baby, acquaintances begin to ask them, "When are you having another one?" I suggest you reply, "When are you leaving?"

That's all the etiquette tips I have room for now, but I have plenty of others. Here are a few you can look forward to learning more about in a future rant:

- Send thank you cards or you may not get a gift next time.

- Don't slam doors; you never know who might be napping.

- Don't ask a woman when her baby is due

unless you're absolutely certain she's pregnant.

- And be kind to everyone you meet; you never know who might win the lottery next.

How to Win Friends
and Remember Their Names

Many years ago, I read *How to Win Friends and Influence People* by Dale Carnegie. All these years later I have some friends but no influence whatsoever. Still, I did pick up a few pointers that I continue to use today. Some of the most useful have to do with remembering names.

Mr. Carnegie advised that when you meet someone new, you should try to use his or her name often in the ensuing conversation. "Nice to meet you, Bill. Isn't the weather nice, Bill? Is that spaghetti sauce on your jacket, Bill?" Meanwhile, look closely at Bill until your mind begins to associate his name with his appearance—or until he says, "I'm not Bill."

According to Dale Carnegie, this was the strategy used by Napoleon the Third, Emperor of France and nephew of that other Napoleon, the French statesman and military leader. Napoleon the Third bragged that despite his busy life as emperor, he could remember the name of every person he'd ever met, which had to be easier back then when so many people were named Napoleon.

We have many more names to remember today and, even using this tip, we may occasionally find ourselves forgetting a name. Mr. Carnegie and Napoleon the Third may have had many friends and vast influence, but they had no suggestions at all for this predicament. So I've come up with my own.

First, before it happens to you again, come to an agreement with your spouse or significant other that if you fail to introduce, it doesn't necessarily mean you lack manners, although you might. It simply means that you can't remember the person's name, and he or she should not press the issue by saying, "Dear, where are your manners?"

Of course, there is a chance that under these

circumstances, the Nameless Face may actually come to your rescue and introduce herself. Then you can say, "I'm sorry! I thought you'd met."

You could also try introducing your spouse and hope that Nameless Face will pipe up with her own name. I'll demonstrate: "This is my husband, (fill in name, which presumably you know)." Then stop. Nameless Face and your spouse will both look at you expectantly, waiting for the other half of the introduction. Smile back at them, but say nothing.

If Nameless Face has any manners at all, she'll jump in after a few seconds of dead air with, "I'm So and So." Then you can say, "I'm sorry. Where are my manners?" This way, So and So will not know that you forgot her name, although she may think you have no manners.

The situation becomes more complex when you encounter Nameless Face/Uncertain Identity. Recently, I ran into a couple at the grocery store who spoke enthusiastically for five minutes about a variety of benign topics including the weather and the joys of grocery shopping. Meanwhile I was thinking, "Who are you, and why are you talking to me?"

The best strategy in this situation is to make a quick escape, but they had me cornered by the frozen foods. So I smiled and encouraged their chatter, sure that if they talked long enough, they would eventually give some clue to their identities. When that didn't happen, I became convinced that they had me confused with someone else. I excused myself, thinking how embarrassed they were going to be when they saw that person the next time. Then as I slipped away, the woman said, "It was good to see you, Dorothy." Lucky guess.

That brings me to the most complex situation of all: Wrong Name/Wrong Person/Wrong Everything. Recently I bumped into an acquaintance. I greeted her warmly, but she remained reserved—even cold. I tried harder. I asked about her family and her work. She backed away. Maybe she didn't remember my name. Or maybe she just didn't like me anymore.

But as she hurried away it hit me: She was not who I thought she was. Not only did she not know my name, she didn't know me. Nor, apparently, did she want to. I guess she's one more person I'll never have any influence over.

Hold the Pickles,
Hold the Cellphone

A cellphone is a wonderful thing in the hands of someone who remembers to charge it. And I'm not just
thinking of the obvious benefits: rescue when you're
stranded. Or your spouse wants you to pick up milk.
Or you want to win a radio call-in contest from the
highway. Or you need to check in with your parole
officer before you leave the state. That sort of thing.

Cellphones also give us valuable insight into
the personal lives of others. For example, not only
have they made it easier for lovers to communicate,

they've made it easier for me to listen in when lovers are communicating. I've been privileged to hear two dramatic lovers' quarrels, one just a few days ago. Of course, I could only hear one side of each of the arguments. But coincidentally, in both cases the person I was hearing was absolutely right.

I once heard a handsome young man making a date on his cellphone, and I was happy to hear that she apparently accepted. I also once heard a not-so-handsome young man breaking a date on his cellphone. Maybe he wasn't any less handsome, but I felt bad for the woman. It was all I could do not to grab that phone out of his hands and tell her, "You can do better!"

Cellphones provide us with entertainment wherever we go, and I'm not talking about watching YouTube videos on them. One day I saw a man riding a bicycle and talking on a cellphone. (Look, Ma! No hands!) Waiting to see if he was going to make it through that intersection was spine tingling. Maybe for him too.

I watched a couple in a local restaurant impatiently waiting for friends. I saw them looking at their watches, and I saw them looking at their watches again. I heard them commenting on the lateness of the hour and on their friends' tardiness habit. And I saw the woman punch her cellphone after they had decided to call their friends and hurry them along. At that very moment, I heard a cellphone ringing from a table across the restaurant.

I was once interrupted just as I was about to deliver the punch line of a joke about cellphones—by a cellphone going off in the front row. The audience will never know, but that beat my punch line.

And one of my favorite benefits of all is that this device that was designed to help us communicate provides us with an easy way to get out of communicating. It's counterintuitive, I know. I stumbled across the technique by accident when a clerk at the convenience store chatted on his cellphone while I waited. And waited and waited. Whatever he was talking about was clearly more important than my paying and being on my way, at least to him. Either I was invisible or he was holding out for the next shift change so that someone else would have to deal with me.

And that's when it hit me. Getting a well-timed phone call could be a great way to avoid an unpleasant social situation. Say the conversation at the family gathering turns political and you don't want to have to tell everyone again why they're all wrong. Or the woman in the kiosk at the mall is preparing to invite you over for an eyebrow plucking you don't want. Or you're pulled over for speeding and the officer is approaching your car. Well, maybe not then.

But generally people leave you alone when you're on the telephone—unless they're under the age of ten. Unfortunately, there's no way to get your cellphone to ring at precisely the right moment. Or is there? The following is purely for demonstration purposes. I haven't tried it—yet.

Let's say I'm at a carnival and I don't feel like being hounded to play Whack-A-Mole. I don't want to pay someone to guess my weight because it would be embarrassing if they guessed right. And I certainly don't want to try the Balloon Dart Throw. It's not that I don't want to win a giant pink teddy bear, but I'm pretty sure the dart tips are dull, the balloons are underinflated and I couldn't hit one even if that weren't the case.

But I feel bad saying no up and down the midway to people who are just trying to make a living. So as I near the Balloon Dart Throw booth, I look surprised and give a little start as though my cellphone has just vibrated in my pocket. I pull it out, tap the screen, put it to my ear, say hello and listen carefully—to nothing.

If I feel confident in my acting abilities, I can say a few words as I pass by the booth, but I don't have to say much. I can just nod and frown. The man at the Balloon Dart Throw booth thinks I'm listening carefully, so he sees no point in calling out to me even though he senses I'm the perfect mark—soft-hearted and a poor thrower.

See how simple it would be to avoid talking to people you'd rather not talk to? I can't believe no one has thought of it yet. Every third person I saw today was talking on the phone. How easy it would be for them to just fake it as I pass by. Hey, wait....

As wonderful as cellphones are, there is much concern that they're contributing to a decline in manners. But anyone who thinks people used to be more thoughtful with their phone usage never heard stories of their elderly relatives listening in on party lines.

Maybe the issue is not so much that manners are declining, but that etiquette hasn't kept pace with technology. The following are my suggestions for proper cellphone etiquette. While I may not always follow them myself, I really wish everybody else would.

1.   Never take pictures of someone else without asking, especially in a locker room.

2.   Never text or talk on the cellphone while you're driving. I admit I have on rare occasions talked on the phone while I was driving. But text and drive? How do you do that? I couldn't text and drive even if you held the wheel for me.

3.   Never carry on a lengthy cellphone conversation with one person while you're having lunch with another—especially if they're buying. I once saw a teenager talking on a cellphone while she was out to dinner with two adults I assumed were her parents. She was positively animated; they were bored. But what a great way to keep up on your children's lives. And what a good time to snitch their French fries.

4.   Keep it down. We all know it's best to wait until we're alone to speak loudly on our cellphones—say when we're in the privacy of our car speeding across town. I'm joking! But when you do find yourself on the phone in a public place where others are forced to listen to the details of your personal life, at least have the courtesy to make the details interesting.

It's true that I'm not as disturbed by having to overhear cellphone conversations as some people are. What really burns me is that I can only hear one side of the conversation. That leaves the other half of the story up to my imagination, and I don't think anyone wants that.

5.   Turn it off. There are some places you should never talk on the phone, no matter how interesting your conversation is. I was at the movie *Bohemian Rhapsody* when someone's cellphone broke into song up front. It was a catchy little instrumental and I probably would have felt like dancing if I hadn't been holding a bucket of popcorn the size of a rain barrel and trying to hear what Rami Malek was saying. When the cellphone's owner finally answered it, he told the caller—and everyone else in the theater—that he was in the middle of a movie, something those of us in the audience were well aware of.

6.   Silence your phone or set it to vibrate at times when even the ring would be inappropriate. I should warn you though: A vibrating phone is a dancing phone, and I happen to know it can dance right off the banister and down the stairs.

Also, there are times when even a vibrating phone

isn't appropriate. For example, the buzzing sound in the middle of a funeral can sound like there's a bee in the church, and that can be very distracting.

And there's a downside to silent cellphones besides the fact that your spouse gets really upset when you don't answer twenty-five calls in a row. It means we can no longer assume that just because the person next to us is speaking, they're speaking to us. I can think of more than one occasion when a good loud ring would have prevented embarrassment—mine.

Recently, as I stood in line at the grocery store, I heard a woman say, "Well, hello!" with all the enthusiasm with which you greet your best friend who's been missing for several years. Had I heard her cellphone ring, I would never have spun around and said, "Hi, there!" with equal enthusiasm. I should have known no one gets that excited when they see the back of my head.

When the woman behind door number three in the restroom spoke, I assumed she was talking to me since I was the only other person present. Being the polite person I am, I said, "I'm sorry. What did you say?" She replied with obvious annoyance, "I wasn't talking to you!" Oh. The caller must have felt really important when they heard the flush.

A man at the grocery store looked right at me and asked, "Do we need cereal?" I wasn't sure it was any of his business but I said, "I've got plenty." That's when I noticed he was using an earpiece.

7. Don't try to carry on a business transaction with one person while you're having a cellphone conversation with another. This isn't just a matter of courtesy; it's a matter of self-protection. If you say "yes" to the fast food worker when she asks if you want fries with that, you may unwittingly be giving your teenager permission to use the car tonight.

Or let's say you're standing in line at the deli counter and at the precise moment it's your turn to order, your cellphone rings. You say, "Hello, dear." Your spouse says "Hi, Sweetie."

The clerk says, "Uh, hi."

You say "hi" back.

The clerk says, "Can I help you?"

You say to your spouse, "Just a minute, honey." The clerk blushes. Your spouse says, "Quick question."

You say, "I said just a minute." The clerk looks hurt.

You say, "I'll take a roast beef on wheat."

Your spouse says, "Do we have any mustard?" at the same time as the clerk says, "Would you like mayo?"

You say to the clerk, "No mayo. Just mustard."

Your spouse says, "We do have mayo, but I don't see any mustard."

You say to your spouse, "Yes, we have mayo. I'll get mustard."

The clerk says, "What?"

You can see how rude it is to carry on a conversation with one person on your cellphone while you're doing business with another. But if you really feel you must, the least you can do is order them sandwiches too.

The World According to Facebook

Oh, look! I'm having a friendversary today. How thoughtful of Facebook to remember that special day three years ago when "Blanche" and I officially became friends on their site. Now…who's Blanche again?

You know how it is. I have so many Facebook friends that I'm reminded of that old adage, "There are no strangers here, only friends you have not met yet." The saying is credited to the poet William Butler Yeats, who as you know was a big fan of Facebook. Unfortunately he died in 1939, just as it was really taking off.

I'm joking. It only *seems* like it's been around that long. In its short life, Facebook has replaced solitaire as the most common way to avoid doing actual work on the computer, created terrific job opportunities for Russian trolls and taken the art of small talk to a whole new level: "I hate rain." "Me too." "I'm doing laundry." "Have fun with that."

It's also given new meaning to the word "friend." Back when I started using Facebook, I wondered what it meant that someone wanted to be my Facebook friend. Would she add me to her Christmas card list? Give me birthday presents? Invite me to lunch? That's one of my favorite things to do with friends.

But I soon learned that having cyber friends is very different than having real friends. For one thing, here in the real world, "friend" is a noun. On Facebook it's also a verb. People friend you, then they unfriend you—sort of like in elementary school.

In the real world, they say a good friend will help you move, but a true friend will help you move a body. I'm going to go out on a limb here and say the vast majority of my Facebook friends wouldn't help me with either one of those, and especially the latter. But if I'm ever in a position to need that kind of help, I probably shouldn't mention it on Facebook.

In the real world, a friend is someone you can tell your deepest thoughts to, trusting they won't tell a million other people. On Facebook you tell a million people yourself, and your friends don't even try to stop you from embarrassing yourself.

Real friends never sit down to dinner with you and start right in discussing politics unless they're pretty sure you agree with them. But I have Facebook friends who post their political views like matadors waving red flags at a bullfight.

Real friends watch your house when you travel and pick you up at the airport when you get back home. Not only do I doubt Blanche could be counted on to do either of those for me, I think she'd be really surprised if I asked her to.

Real friends share everything from gossip to clothing to French fries off each other's plates. I've taken a good look at Blanche's photo and I think I'll recognize her if I ever run into her at a restaurant. But I bet if I walk over to her table and say, "Happy friendversary, Blanche! I really love your cat video posts," she won't offer me a French fry. Or loan me an outfit.

Facebook friends do share though. Boy, do they share. I have a few Facebook friends whose posts I know I'll look back on someday and see as warning signs I missed.

The husband of a Facebook friend just posted photos of her giving birth. For the baby's sake, I hope they're still married.

And lately there's been a rash of photos of, well, rashes on Facebook. Also bruises, sores and open wounds. See right there. My friend "Karen" just shared a photo of her stitches. A picture is worth a thousand words, but in this case three would have been plenty: "I have stitches."

Sure, we can take down a post, but not always before it takes us down. That's why I think there are a few things we should refrain from posting. No PUI for one thing—you know, posting under the influence. It's amazing how many underage drinkers think this is a good idea and even more shocking how many adults do. Worldwide more than 1.5 billion people log onto Facebook every day, but in an alcoholic haze it's easy for some people to forget their parents, children and employer may be among them.

And I don't think you should ever say something to someone on Facebook that you wouldn't say to their face. Just my luck, I'll tell someone they're a few posts short of a whole fence, then run into them at the grocery store the next day.

I don't think you should ever post about how much you hate your job either. Your employer may find out and relieve you of your pain. In fact "Mark's" comments about his job lead me to believe he's going to need another one very soon. Unfortunately, if potential employers check him out on Facebook, he may get to spend the rest of his days unemployed and posting from his mother's basement.

None of this is to say I don't enjoy Facebook. I love animal videos and baby pictures. I love reconnecting with people I haven't seen in years. I like that people aren't as choosy about Facebook friends as they are in the real world so I can have more of them. Plus I know some interesting people on Facebook, although, as I've already established, "know" might be too strong a word.

One Facebook friend travels a lot. She just posted a dozen photos of her Hawaiian honeymoon and they are beautiful. Hey, wait. She's on what should be the best vacation of her life with the person she presumably loves more than anyone in the world, and she's staring at her phone. I have half a mind to comment, "Don't tell us you love him to the moon and back. Tell him. He's right there." I don't though.

He's probably looking at his phone too. She'd have to send him a Facebook message to get his attention.

It's not my problem. I type "awesome photos" and scroll down. New car—like. Cute puppy—love. Fresh wound—stop it.

Wow! That looks good though. My friend just made a Chocolate Sformato—a baked chocolate pudding—with amaretto whipped cream and little chocolate sprinkles on top. It looks fabulous. And I don't get to taste it.

That friend looks exactly like she did when we were in high school except with better hair. And that one is jetting off to Europe. I bet I don't even get a postcard. Those are so 90s. Besides she's got more than a thousand friends. That would be a lot of postcards. And a lot of friendversaries.

Look at them—they're in a hot air balloon. I'm amazed they have cell service. And me? I'm sitting here reading about it all. Not as fun maybe, but I always have service in my house.

That friend just ran a marathon. That one went skydiving. That one was named Mother of the Year. I'm impressed…also boring and inadequate. Sigh. Looking at Facebook is like being in cyber middle school.

Maybe I'm coming down with FOMO—Fear of Missing Out. I read about it on the internet, so it must be real. FOMO is that "blend of anxiety, inadequacy and irritation" that flares up when we see all the exciting things other people are doing while we sit around reading about it on social media. Ironically, sitting around reading about it might be part of the reason we're missing out.

Another article listed the following symptoms for something called Facebook Syndrome:

1. Comparing your life with the lives of your Facebook friends.

How could I not do that? I can't even say "Sformato," let alone make it.

2. Having unrealistic perceptions of your friends' happiness.

There's always someone richer, thinner and driving a nicer car than me, just like outside of Facebook. And there are all those pictures of smiling people. It's easy to forget that just because someone is smiling, it doesn't mean they like everyone else in the picture.

3. Obsessing about other people's daily activities.

Geez, I wonder how that dessert was. Look at

that. She's running another 10K. No wonder she looks so good. Hey, they were in town, and they didn't even call.

4. Experiencing anxiety if you cannot check your newsfeed at regular intervals.

This explains why we stare at our handheld devices while we're walking, eating and driving down the interstate at seventy-five miles an hour.

Do you suppose it means something that we never post pictures of ourselves sitting in front of our computers looking at Facebook? Put down that device. Back away from that computer. Go make your own Chocolate Sformato. And bring me some...friend.

Modern
Love

One Friday morning when I was a freshman in college, a certain nice young man asked me on a date for that evening. I agreed without hesitation. There was just one problem. Another not-as-nice young man had already asked me out—sort of. His exact words had been, "Maybe we'll go out Friday night." And I had agreed that maybe we would.

I realized I had a problem as soon as the second "yes" was out of my mouth. (In my defense, let me say I was young, not very bright and not accustomed to being asked out by one man, let alone two.)

I stewed about my dilemma all morning and finally sought the advice of my roommate, the beautiful Melanie, who was used to having more than one date on the same night. Her sage advice took the form of an insightful question: "Which one is cuter?"

They were both equal in that regard but, as I said, one was nice and the other was not as nice. So I screwed up my courage and dialed Not So Nice's number intending to cancel the date we may not have even had. No answer and no answering machine. Also no cellphone, no email, no Twitter, no Instagram, no Snapchat and no Facebook. I was in college in the eighties; we were lucky to have telephones.

I tried several more times that day without success. That left me to call Very Nice to cancel. Wouldn't you know it; he answered on the first ring. How does one say, "I would like to go out with you but I can't because, before you asked me, I'd already said okay when someone equally as attractive but not nearly as nice said maybe we should go out, and it would be really awkward if you both showed up at my door at the same time"?

One doesn't. One lies about having relatives

in town. Or at least this one did. Very Nice hung up and we never spoke again. I'm sure he would consider it poetic justice that Not So Nice never did follow up on his maybe.

I haven't thought about that incident in years, but the memory came back to me like a bounced email when I overheard a young man at the grocery store canceling a date on his cellphone. There he stood, surrounded by snack foods, saying he wasn't feeling well, which may or may not have been true. He was at the grocery store after all and not in the aspirin aisle. But instead of looking down on him, I was thinking, "I wish we'd had cellphones when I was single." I wanted to march over to him and tell him how easy he had it. I didn't though, because I didn't want him to know I was listening in.

Today anyone dumb enough to get herself into a predicament like I did could easily cancel one or the other date via cellphone, email or social media. She could text it, tweet it, or hire an airplane and write it across the sky. My only options were landline and carrier pigeon.

I have a cellphone and email myself now, and I'm on Facebook and Twitter. And I rarely have reason to cancel a date these days, though I have been temped when my husband checks his email while we're out to dinner.

But the whole thing inspires me to consider the many ways technology has made romance more efficient, if not more romantic. For example, in my dating days young men asked young ladies for their telephone numbers—other young ladies anyway. Today a guy could walk away with a cellphone number, an email address, a street address, a Twitter handle and a website URL. A woman's contact information could take up three pages in a little black book if anyone had little black books anymore.

Potential couples can also check out each other's blogs or meet each other on Facebook, Snapchat or Instagram. Of course, there's always the chance that she's fifteen posing as twenty-five and he has a criminal record and wives in three states. But still, how convenient.

Getting to know each other is easier today too. A young couple can text message each other from across the classroom all day. They shouldn't but they can—until their cellphones are confiscated.

There are some drawbacks though. For one thing, messaging someone on Instagram to tell him you're breaking a date might be considered rude and would likely ensure that you never get another chance with him.

Besides that, there are so many places to check for messages these days that your recipient may not even see you've canceled until he stumbles across your message while sitting patiently, staring at his smartphone waiting for you to arrive for your rendezvous. By the time I listen to my voice messages and read my email, snail mail, Facebook and Twitter messages and the Post-it notes stuck on my office door, I'm exhausted and it's time to start all over.

And the number of ways we have to communicate hasn't improved the quality of communication one bit. If I'd had a smartphone and voice command back in college, I may have texted Not So Nice something like, "Wasn't sure if we were getting together or not so I made other plans." But it may have come out something like, "Washing sure gather tuna so I evade otter plans." To which he may have replied articulately, "???" Post-it Notes may be our best bet.

The language of love has also changed. Long ago, we had to read between the lines of our love letters: "Did he write carefully with thought and feeling, trying to find the exact words to show his love? Or did he dash his letter off during commercials, as if I meant nothing to him?" Today, emoticons make an email's true meaning clear: "It was wonderful to see you! ;-)" Or, "I miss you sooooo much! :-("

And there are many romantic instant message abbreviations available for young couples, for example the very dreamy "MOS," which loosely translated means, "Gotta go. Mom is looking over my shoulder."

Lake
Heyhowareya

I'm trudging across a slushy parking lot when an acquaintance hurries by and says, "Hi! How are you?" I say, "Great! How are you?" like I just won the lottery. Except I didn't. And I'm not great either.

I recently had minor foot surgery. My foot hurts, the medical bills are starting to roll in and a surgical shoe isn't ideal for tromping through ice and snow. I know because I've been wearing this one for a month. It's black, open-toed and very attractive. I'm joking. A surgical shoe makes an army boot look dainty. One size doesn't quite fit all—but one shoe does fit either foot. How attractive can that be?

So no, I'm not fine. Nor do I particularly care how she is at the moment.

She's also fine or at least she says she is, and then she hurries by. We could have just said hello. That's what we meant. But I can't just say hello. In fact, when I greet someone, what I usually say is, "Hey, how are ya," except it's one long word—"heyhoware-eya," like a lake in Hawaii.

Almost everyone I know greets other people with some version of "how are you"—"how's it goin'," "how ya doin'," "how the heck are you"—whether they want to know or not.

And almost everyone I know has a pat response: "Fine." "Good." "Great!" A few people have more creative answers: "I'm so good it should be illegal." Or "If I were any better, I could be arrested." I want to smack them. Then they wouldn't be fine.

The whole ritual is so automatic that I can envision my coming across someone who's just fallen off a ladder and saying, "Heyhowareya." Worse, I can see her answering, "I'm fine. Could you call an ambulance, please?"

I know some people think "Have a good day"

and it's many variations—have a good one, a nice day, a great day, a blessed day—are equally meaningless. I disagree. When I say, "Have a good day," I mean it. I want everyone to have a good day. People having good days are so much easier to get along with.

My most clichéd pleasantry is "I'm sorry." I first became aware of how often I say it when we had a Japanese exchange student. She was confused when I offered condolences to someone by saying "I'm sorry," because only moments before, she'd heard me say "I'm sorry" when I meant, "Pardon me, I didn't hear what you said." She'd also heard me say, "I'm sorry" when I meant, "Forgive me. I stepped on your foot." Taken in that context, I can understand her confusion. My saying "I'm sorry" about a death might have sounded to her like I was confessing I had something to do with it.

But I'm getting off track. I'm sorry about that. There's probably no harm in the practice of saying "I'm sorry," "have a good one" or "how are you?" We can safely assume that most of the time "how are you" is the equivalent of saying "hello" and that "fine" is just another way to say "hi" back. Most of us are aren't expecting honesty when we ask someone how they are, nor are we always honest when we're asked. If we were, our response might be something like, "You really want to know how I am? You don't have that kind of time."

But maybe we could be more honest on both sides of the question. We could say, "I don't have time to talk so I'm not going to ask how you are, but I really do care."

Then they might say, "No problem. You can buy me lunch later and we'll talk."

Or if we do have time, we might say, "How are you—really?"

And they could answer, "I'd be better if my shoulder wasn't acting up, my kids behaved and I had more money in my bank account."

"Tell me more. Let's start with your shoulder."

You do see this kind of honesty occasionally. Once at the grocery store I greeted a man I barely know with my standard, "Heyhowareya?" And he said, "Not well. Not well at all." And by the time I finally left him, neither was I.

Maybe more than honesty we need awareness. If he'd been more aware, the man at the grocery store might have noticed that my ice cream was melting while he filled me in on why he wasn't well.

I recently saw an acquaintance who I'd heard has

been quite ill. If I'd been paying more attention, I might have asked, "How are you doing?" in a gentle way, like a friend, instead of "Heyhowareya," with all the enthusiasm of a game show host.

I really do want to know how you are when I have the time to listen, and if it's not well, I want to know exactly why. I'm snoopy that way.

As for me, I'm okay but I'll be better when I can wear my regular shoe again. And yes, I realize you didn't ask. But I know you will the next time I see you.

CHAPTER FIVE

What Is the Matter with Everyone?

A Little Birdie Told Me I Need to Get Out More

I have a cat and I have a canary and watching them is more entertaining than writing and possibly more entertaining than reading what I've written too. But this morning, after spending a fair amount of time sitting at my computer watching my pets instead of writing, I had the following brilliant insight: I need to get out more.

I need to travel, see the world and experience new things. My pets don't travel much nor do I want them to, but their sheltered existence gives them a skewed view of the world. And maybe mine does too—the way a fish in a fishbowl thinks the ocean is tiny and has a glass wall all the way around it.

Mr. Tweeters—he's the canary, but you probably guessed that—has lived in a cage his whole life. And for most of that time, the cage has been in the same bay window in my office. I'm sure he thinks this room is the entire world, though he's never actually said so.

On one side of his cage is a window that I admit could be washed more often. On the other side, there are stacks of office clutter. The sun rises and sets at widely different times every day. It all depends on what time I get around to putting the blanket on the cage for the night and removing it the next morning. From Tweeters' viewpoint, it's a jungle out there.

But as far as he knows, the other creatures in the jungle are fairly benign, though they can't sing worth a darn. But then he hasn't seen—or heard— many creatures. Mostly he sees me sitting here by the computer muttering and the cat lounging beside the bird cage. Despite the fact that he's just inches away from a predator, Tweeters goes about his business unconcerned. It's like if I trusted lions just because I've never been attacked at a zoo.

Sebastian—the cat—is somewhat more leery of other creatures and for good reason. He has twice been chased through our home by large dogs who were visiting us. One was a black lab who only wanted to play and the other was a red heeler who only wanted to swallow him whole. Being unable to tell the difference, Sebastian has decided no visitor can be trusted.

He has traveled a bit more than the bird, but he hasn't really enjoyed it. Once when he was a kitten, he tried to travel out of the garage at the precise moment the door was coming down. He wasn't hurt, but he decided then and there that he doesn't care for travel, at least via the garage. That's like if I decided to give up flying after surviving a plane crash which, come to think of it, I probably would.

My husband and I reinforce Sebastian's travel fears by occasionally forcing him into the car and taking him to the vet's office. That is never a pleasant experience for him and he has a way of making it pretty unpleasant for us too.

Not only that, as far as he knows the world is a violent and frightening place, at least when you leave through the garage. He's content to stay in his little neighborhood—my house—where everyone loves him, the temperature is always between 68 and 72 degrees and there's a treat jar.

If my pets ever bolted out the back door and took off exploring on their own, they'd soon learn that both temperatures and food supplies vary considerably. And they'd discover that some creatures are dangerous, others are friendly and plenty of them sing better than the one sitting at the computer every day.

Yes, these are the things I think about when I tell my family not to disturb me because I'm working. I told you—I definitely need to get out more.

What Is the Matter
with Everyone

I like my drinks ice cold or scalding hot, nothing in between—except tomato juice which I like at room temperature. I like tea but I don't care for coffee. And I like iced tea better than hot tea, except when I'm chilly. I'm often chilly even in the summer because some people turn their air conditioners higher than I think should be legal.

No, I'm not nuts, though I do like nuts—any kind. But I like pistachios and almonds best and cashews least. That's lucky because cashews are both my husband's and my son's favorite. My family gets along fine with a can of mixed nuts, which some would say is a fitting metaphor.

I'm not telling you all this because I aspire to be one of those celebrities making demands for my dressing room. But since you asked, I'd like red roses, a radio tuned to NPR and diet cola. I want the cola over crushed—not cubed—ice, and I'd prefer it from a fountain, not a plastic bottle. Either Pepsi or Coke is fine though. I'm not picky. And neither one has agreed to endorse me.

No, the reason I'm telling you all this is because I'm intrigued by preferences. If I could get a research grant to study something, I would study why other people like what they like and not what I like. Is everyone except me deeply flawed? It's fascinating.

I doubt I could get a research grant though, because I can't see a foundation thinking this is as important as I do, plus I'm not a researcher. What I am is particular and curious.

For example, I'm particular about not putting salt on my watermelon and curious about why some people do. On the other hand, some people like salt on their tomatoes (me), and some people think that's a waste of tomatoes and salt. They might even sprinkle sugar on their tomatoes, which I consider completely irrational.

Is it nature? Are their taste buds simply inferior to mine? Or is it nurture? Did their mothers think a spoon full of sugar would make the vegetables go down? (Yes, I know tomatoes are fruits, but I prefer to think of them as vegetables.)

In keeping with my ice cold and scalding hot preference, I believe it's never too hot for soup and never too cold for ice cream. But I have a relative who turns his nose up at soup, behavior I consider un-American. And given the choice, he would choose any other dessert over ice cream. If he can't be trusted to choose rocky road over angel food, how can he be trusted at all?

I used to lunch with a friend who always carefully removed all the onions, peppers and tomatoes from her salad and then gave them to me. I'd watch her doing this and think, "What is wrong with you?" But I kept my opinion to myself because that's the kind of person I am. Plus I was happy to get her onions, peppers and tomatoes.

I know someone who doesn't like her food to touch. Her potatoes must never touch her meat loaf, and neither one must ever touch her green beans.

Meanwhile, I purposely take a little of each on my fork, so I can chew them altogether. It's quicker so I have a better chance of getting seconds. Plus it tastes better. Why can't she see it my way?

It isn't just food, of course. Some people are shoe store people. Some people are furniture store people. I'm an office supply store gal myself. I go there often for the printer cartridges but I stay to gaze at the pens, markers and highlighters. And I love planners like a hardware store person loves light fixtures.

And so it goes. Some people are car people and some people are truck people. Some people are dog people and some people are cat people. Some people are morning people, some people are night people, and some people aren't people at all except for an hour or two around dinner time.

But every one of them has at least one thing in common. They didn't consult me when they were deciding what kind of people to be. What is the matter with everyone?

Fish Sticks and
World Peace

Sometimes in the midst of chaos and calamity, I'm overcome with an uncharacteristic urge to step ahead of the troubled masses and shout a few wise words of comfort: Help! Somebody, do something!

I'm kidding. I know it's up to us. It stinks but somehow we're going to have to muddle through together. And naturally that brings me to the subject of fish sticks.

I'm no biblical scholar, which will become obvious very quickly, but I've always liked the story of the feeding of the 5,000. Maybe you're familiar with it. It was getting close to meal time and the disciples wanted Jesus to send the crowd that was following them to the villages to buy food. That's exactly how I react when I have company. "Let's eat out."

But Jesus was having none of it. He told the disciples to feed the people themselves. I'm sure they had that same inadequate feeling I get when I have unexpected guests and all I have in the house is a couple of cans of cream of mushroom soup and some shriveled potatoes.

Unfortunately the disciples were only able to scare up five loaves of bread and a couple of fish, and they couldn't just order pizza—not for that many people.

As the story goes, Jesus broke the bread, the disciples passed it out and voila; not only did they feed everyone, they picked up twelve baskets full of leftovers. That's what I call wonder bread!

Actually what I call it is mystical mathematics or divine multiplication, and I could have used it back in algebra class.

Here's how I think of it. Everybody has something to offer, and if we all used what we have fully and only for good, and if we got out of the way and let other people do the same, the sum of all of those parts would add up to a big wonderful whole. We've already established that math is not my strong suit, but it does seem like a nice idea, don't you think?

I've always seen the loaves and fish as a metaphor for everything we have—not just our resources, but our time and talents, our gifts. With good intentions and a little divine intervention, maybe we could feed 5,000 too, metaphorically speaking. The impact of our actions could spread like ripples in a pond, seeds from a cottonwood tree or flu germs in an elementary school.

I don't have five loaves and two fish, but I might have a couple of fish sticks. You were wondering when I was going to get to that, weren't you? I write. I vote. I give money—and blood, which I have more of.

And there are people with bigger fish to fry. They teach, heal, lead others and create cool stuff. The way I see it, some people have a whole halibut and loaf of multi-grain. We need it all; the king salmon and the catfish, the day-old bagels and the hamburger buns. And we need it all the time, not just when we...uh... flounder. Sorry.

It gives me hope when I see people using their

gifts, whatever they are; when they play the cards they've been dealt, strum the strings they've been strung with, share the fish sticks in their freezer. Forgive me, I'm the queen of the mixed metaphor. It's one of my gifts.

If every single person used their talents and resources fully and only for good, I imagine the world would be about as perfect as it could be. "Only for good" is the operative phrase though. Financial geniuses who bilk people out of their retirement funds or computer whizzes who use their abilities to steal identities ought to have their talents revoked and given to someone who will use them more responsibly. Me, for example. Neither of those skills are among my fish sticks and I could really use them.

So you do whatever it is you do and I'll do whatever it is I do. At this point you may be thinking, "What exactly is that?" I wonder myself sometimes. But I've been writing for a few years now and I've written about a lot of things. Maybe I've encouraged a few people to pay attention to where they park, check their texts before they send them and avoid getting carried away with a new paper shredder. Maybe I've reminded someone to remove the original gift tag before they re-gift or kept them from getting on an ancient elevator with a full bladder. I figure if I've persuaded even one woman to refrain from applying lipstick until the Novocain wears off, my life will not have been in vain.

Jobs I
Couldn't Do

I watched the veterinarian give my growling cat a shot and I thought to myself, "Well there's a job I wouldn't want."

I had the same thought when I noticed that long ago workers braver than I am had worked right up to the edge of the Grand Canyon to build a low wall beside it. And when I watched a truck driver back up an eighteen-wheeler in a full parking lot while we all watched to see if he could do it without hitting our cars. He could and he did. Some of us can't do as well with a compact car.

I always spend Labor Day contemplating work, which I find much easier than doing it. I think about how society needs everyone's contributions and how it's right to appreciate everyone for the work they do, as long as it's legal. And I think about how I'd like to pay tribute to all the people who do jobs I couldn't or wouldn't do, but this book isn't that long.

So let me highlight just a few of them. For starters I would never want one of those jobs that require you to stay calm under pressure. For example, first responders, emergency room doctors and playground teachers.

Of all the professions that require calm and patience, driver education teacher must be right up there with hostage negotiator. I have none of either so I delegated the responsibility of teaching my son to drive to a professional—driver education teacher, not hostage negotiator.

I wouldn't want a job that required precision either. I'm more of a "that's close enough" kind of person, and that doesn't work if you're building bridges, doing brain surgeries or rigging parachutes.

Sure actors on the big screen are amazing, but what about actors on TV commercials? Now there's a tough job. How do you keep a straight face when you have to dress up like a mustard bottle or say things like "Thanks, Baseboard Buddy" while gazing lovingly at a dust mop?

I sleep almost as well in a moving vehicle as I do in a bed, so I probably wouldn't make much of a bus driver. I am a pretty good driver—when I'm awake, but that is one of the qualities you look for in a good bus driver.

I appreciate fast food workers at busy drive-through windows. No matter how long the line, they still get my order right. And honestly sometimes when I order a salad and iced tea, I wish they'd goof and give me someone's bacon burger, large fries and chocolate shake.

And I've long admired people who work in those sandwich shops where they wrap sandwiches so perfectly they look like professionally-wrapped gifts. I once had a job that required I wrap gifts, and they were always a little lumpy. It's so much easier to toss a gift into a gift bag, but you probably shouldn't do that with a six-inch meatball sub and all the fixings.

Some of the hardest working people in our country don't even get Labor Day off. Caregivers, for example. They work hard and their pay isn't always that great. And their lives would be a lot easier if people only needed care between 8:00 a.m. and 5:00 p.m. Monday through Friday and never on holidays. To the people they care for and their families, caregivers are more important than bankers, senators or NFL quarterbacks.

I admire people who deal with customers all day and do it cheerfully and efficiently. That includes receptionists, retail staff, wait staff and others. I've been on both sides of the customer service equation—a customer and a customer service person—and I've always found it easier to be the customer. But my customers may not have felt that way.

I was a server when I was in high school. And when you wait tables, the size of your income depends entirely on how friendly, efficient and awake you are all day, every day. I happen to know that when you're tired yourself, it's hard to be friendly to people who haven't had their coffee yet.

I have great respect for teachers. There are few professions more important to the future of our country than educators. I'm a mom. I love children. But for me, standing in front of a classroom all day would be like standing in the middle of a popcorn popper that could start popping at any minute.

I admire daycare workers too. I worked in a daycare as part of a class I took in college. It was only one semester long, but that was long enough to convince me that childcare was not the job for me. It was long enough to convince the children, too.

I admire people who fix things, like mechanics, service people and marriage counselors, though I suppose the only people who can fix a marriage are the people it belongs to. Thank goodness that's not the case for cars and washing machines. (I still admire marriage counselors though.)

Speaking of washing machines, ours was too far gone for a repairman. And now I have a lot of respect for furniture movers and delivery people. Two delivery guys wrestled our new washing machine out of their truck and lugged it through our garage and into our tiny laundry room without hurting themselves, breaking anything or swearing even once. Even more impressive, they had the good manners not to gasp when they saw how dirty the floor was beneath the old one.

There are some professionals I admire so much I'd like them to move right into my basement. One is a computer person. When I worked in an office

I could call on our highly-trained computer staff when I had computer problems. When I have similar difficulties in my home office, all I have at my disposal is a hammer and some salty language.

I'd like a housekeeper to move into my basement too. She could clean up after the computer person—and me. And I do appreciate people who clean up after other people. Custodians, housekeepers and sanitation workers all do the kind of work that we completely take for granted unless they don't do it well.

I cleaned cabins in Yellowstone National Park one summer while I was in college and I learned to appreciate people who do the job for longer than a summer. It's hard work. It requires attention to detail and commitment to quality. Plus there are all those beds and you can't even take a nap.

I'd like a proofreader to move in too. That would save me trouble and save my readers confusion. I once wrote about buying a raffle ticket for an afghan except, without thinking, I capitalized Afghan. It looked like instead of a handmade blanket, I was hoping to win a person from Afghanistan, and for just one dollar. As it turns out I didn't win either one. An afghan would have been nice, but an Afghan could have cooked the food of their homeland. That would have been helpful with all those extra people living in my basement.

The Coolest Generation

The first people ever to make disparaging remarks about the younger generation were Adam and Eve and for good reason; Cain and Abel never could get along.

But every generation since has found fault with the next one. I hate to break it to you but complaining about "kids nowadays" is the first sign of aging. Besides, as somebody smarter than me once put it, "Those who criticize the younger generation forget who raised it."

The second sign of aging is romanticizing the "good old days." Adam and Eve did that too, and who can blame them?

"Remember back in the garden, Eve?"

"Yeah! I loved that place—except for the snakes."

"I didn't care for the apples either."

The rest of us don't have anything quite like the Garden of Eden to reminisce about, but we still get nostalgic. I've seen a handful of social media posts lately that show both of these symptoms of aging, and they didn't come from Adam and Eve. I feel compelled to address this issue because to my way of thinking, a handful is an epidemic.

The posts rant about how past generations were not only smarter but tougher, which is, of course, true. I'm joking. Whether it's true or not, the way the creators of these diatribes choose to make their point is not helping their cause. One of the emails implies that because we weren't afraid to eat raw hamburger and we rode our bikes without wearing helmets, among other things, we must be tougher. When I was a child, I personally engaged in both behaviors, now considered risky. But the main reason I didn't wear a bike helmet is because you could hardly find them then. And hamburger is produced and processed somewhat differently these days. Would sampling it raw now make me tougher or dumber? Don't answer that.

The writer of one of the other emails implies that we were somehow better children because we didn't play computer games and we swam in lakes instead of swimming pools. But today's children are only using the inventions created and perfected by generations before them. You can't blame them for that. If I'd had a computer when I was a child, I probably would have played computer games too—if I could have figured out how.

And yes, I swam in a lake but that's because I didn't have access to a pool. If I had I'm sure I'd have swum in it, especially that summer we found the dead cow in the lake.

The author of one of the posts I read recently implies that his childhood was superior, in part because when he was young nurses wore hats, he wore high-top Keds and cellphones hadn't been invented yet. I'm not sure I ever owned a pair of high tops. I don't care whether nurses wear hats or not. But that summer day when I was seventeen and stranded on a lonely highway with car troubles, I really could have used a cellphone. Or a nurse with a car.

Waxing nostalgic about the good old days may simply be a symptom of age-related memory loss. Nostalgia is, after all, the overwhelming sense that everything was better if it happened so long ago we can't remember it. How good could the good old days have been if we were eating raw hamburger and smacking our heads on the pavement every time we wrecked our bikes?

It's helpful to remember that back while we were living in whatever era we think of as the "good old days," someone else was calling a previous era the "good old days." Even more remarkable, someday our children will call these days the "good old days." Then they'll start criticizing the next generation, and that's when we'll know they're old.

They're already criticizing us. If Adam and Eve were the first to criticize the next generation for their music, fashion, work ethic and inexperience, Cain and Abel were the first to criticize the last one for being hopelessly out of touch, as though they alone were "cool" and would be the first and only generation to remain that way forever.

And so it goes, generation after generation, like some hereditary disease, young people forgetting they stand on the shoulders of the geezers who came before them and older people forgetting the whippersnappers will soon be running things, possibly better than they did but certainly no worse.

That's why I wasn't surprised to see the following article in my internet news feed recently: "25 Tragically Uncool Things Baby Boomers Won't Let Die." But I was surprised to find there were actually sixty-five items on the list, which suggests that proofreading might be one of the things the authors find tragically uncool.

They didn't mention their names, maybe fearing their grandmothers would stop sending them birthday money. Nor did they say what generation they belong to—X, Y or Z. I'm sure in their minds that goes without saying. It's the cool one.

To call wallpaper, throw pillows and Mrs. Dash tragically uncool seems a bit overdramatic. And the authors are prone to sweeping generalizations too. As I read their "list of things that baby boomers think are cool, but they so aren't," I realized that I, an actual baby boomer, don't find most of them cool at all—or tragically uncool for that matter.

I'm a live-and-let-live kind of person myself, which I think is one of my cooler qualities. And while I don't own them myself, if someone wants to wear an air brushed T-shirt, denim shorts and Crocs, I'm blissfully neutral about it, as I am about golf, scripted wall art and Yahoo.

I don't even own a tragically uncool landline anymore, though I wish I did every time I misplace my cellphone somewhere in my house, which is fairly often.

I don't play racquetball either, but I think anyone who puts their smartphone down long enough to exercise is pretty cool.

I also don't type messages in all capital letters, another allegedly uncool sin of baby boomers. You'll notice I haven't used all caps once in this entire piece. SO THERE!

I do occasionally shop in malls which are, according to the authors, tragically uncool since they buy whatever they want online. I have two words for them: Orange Julius. Besides, malls are staffed with people, some of them very cool, who need jobs.

I've been known to iron, but not because I think it's cool. I do it when my clothes look like I slept in them which is not cool at all.

I'll be happy to let email die and learn the next cool thing, but cool or not, people keep emailing me, so I keep emailing them back because not responding when someone is trying to reach me is rude and rude isn't cool in any generation.

I have neither the time nor the energy to discuss them all, but I will say that of all sixty-five items on the list of twenty-five tragically uncool things baby boomers supposedly love, there were only a few I'd go so far as to call cool. My husband and I celebrated our 30th anniversary with a cruise and I say don't knock it till you've tried it. Anyone who thinks meatloaf is uncool never ate my mom's, though it's possible they ate mine. And I enjoy an episode of NCIS now and then; it gives me something to watch while I iron.

Somewhere between tragically uncool juice from concentrate and paying bills the old fashioned way, the authors managed to blame baby boomers for the Social Security predicament, though we don't find that any cooler than they do

I'd advise them to start saving for retirement because whether they believe it nor not, they'll be older and uncool someday too. But the cool part about getting older is you no longer worry so much about being cool. And that's a good thing because there's an entire generation coming up behind you, ready to tell just how uncool you are—exactly like you once did to someone else.

I Could
Be Wrong

I absently swat at a fly buzzing inside my car as I wait for my turn to use the ATM. The man ahead of me must have seen the swat but not the fly. Apparently he interprets my gesture as impatience with him for being too slow because he gives me a certain unmistakable gesture. Then he drives away and I'll never get the chance to tell him that I didn't think he was slow at all. I think he's vulgar, quick to jump to conclusions and as dumb as a bag of cotton balls, but I didn't think he was slow.

Maybe it's just as well I didn't get a chance to speak my mind because it's possible his gesture wasn't meant for me any more than mine was meant for him. (Also he might have a gun.)

Maybe there was a pesky fly in his car too. Or maybe he was angry at his passenger or at the ATM for saying his account was overdrawn. Now I'll never know unless he reads this and takes the time to write.

These experiences lead me to consider how often, from hundreds of possible explanations, we choose the one that makes us the most disgusted. Or at least I do. And I think other people do too, considering how often they're disgusted with me.

I remember taking my mother to the grocery store many years ago. I hung her handicapped parking emblem on my mirror and helped her walk the few steps to the entrance. Then I ran back to get the list I'd forgotten. Just then two men walked out of the store. They pointed at the handicap parking sign and grumbled something I didn't understand. I assumed they were pointing out that I, whom they had just seen jogging across the parking lot, was parked in a handicap spot. I guess it's possible I was the one misreading the situation. Maybe they were annoyed at the price of cereal.

People probably wondered why I didn't keep my dog on a leash. I'm sure they were judging me because I didn't clean up after him when he did his business on their lawns. They probably thought I was irresponsible for not calling him off when he got into a tussle with another dog. But the truth is I couldn't have if I'd wanted to; I didn't know his name. I liked him; he liked me. But truthfully we'd never met until the morning he decided to follow me on my walk.

But then again, maybe it's me jumping to conclusions. Maybe all those people watching us were admiring what they thought was my handsome pet. Or maybe they were admiring me in my baggy grey sweatpants. Or maybe they were wondering why I stole their dog.

We'd be wise to give each other the benefit of the doubt before we jump to conclusions. When an acquaintance doesn't return your greeting on the street, you might conclude she's snooty and egotistical. But maybe she's too absorbed in her thoughts to notice you. Or maybe she just doesn't like you.

Suppose your spouse forgets your birthday. You might assume he's thoughtless. But maybe he's preoccupied planning your surprise anniversary cruise. Or maybe he doesn't want to remind you of your age.

Suppose I don't keep my house clean. You might assume I'm a slob. But maybe I'm just insanely busy. Or maybe I have health problems. Or maybe it's none of your business.

It's always worth considering all possible explanations for another person's behavior before we judge them harshly. After we've done this compassionately and methodically, there's still plenty of time go ahead and judge them harshly.

One day I was cruising down the interstate with my radio cranked up. A white pickup whizzed by me, pulled back into the right-hand lane and slowed down like the driver just forgot what he was doing.

I hollered, "Don't you have cruise control, buddy? Set it and forget it!" He didn't hear me. I do have cruise control, and I always set it and forget it. So it didn't take me long to catch up. I passed him and gave him my "mean look." I wasn't worried about retaliation; my mean look probably isn't that mean. Plus I have the confidence that comes with tinted windows.

I got back into the driving lane and all was well for ten minutes or so, until the white pickup speeded by me again. I'm not a competitive person. In fact I avoid competition altogether because I hate to lose. But honestly I would have been fine if he'd passed me and kept on going. But no. He slowed down again. It's like he wanted to be close to me.

I held out as long as I could but eventually my cruise control and I caught up, so I passed again. This time I got a good look at the driver as I was going by. And I could clearly see he was one of *those* people: the ones whose sole purpose in life is to irritate me—or you. You know the kind. They wake up in the morning, pull your name out of a hat and set out to wreck your day.

I figured he was the type who speeds up just so he can beat everyone else to the stoplight and takes up two parking spaces so he won't get a dent in his vehicle and leaves his shopping cart in the middle of the parking lot because he doesn't care if anyone else gets a dent in theirs.

I imagined he was the kind of guy who takes the last paper towel and doesn't bother to get more from the closet and doesn't wipe his feet on a snowy day and tosses his litter on the street because he thinks his mother is going to come by later and pick up after him.

I was just getting warmed up when the white pickup passed me again. Yup, I decided. He was definitely that kind of guy. I hadn't noticed it before, but this time I could see he had one those bumper stickers with itty-bitty print you can't read. It probably said, "If you can read this, you're too close."

I figured he makes his living as a spammer. And he probably moonlights at a fake call center where they call during dinner to tell you there's a problem with your credit card or your computer or the IRS. "Take that, you spammer!" And I passed him again.

Yeah, he was definitely the kind of guy who texts when he drives and spits gum on the sidewalk. And I was pretty sure he doesn't call his parents often enough.

I hoped he wasn't going where I was going because I imagined he was one of those people who slams their hotel room door no matter what time of the day or night it is.

There he went again, passing me and slowing down, oblivious to the annoyance he was causing everyone else on the road.

And then I thought, "Wait. Where's the bumper sti…?"

Oh. It was a different white truck.

Take That,
You Misguided Fool

I've only unfriended one person on Facebook, and he had it coming. It was shortly before the last election, and Misguided Fool (not his real name) posted a steady stream of mean-spirited phooey. I realize that on Facebook one person's phooey is another person's enlightened entertainment, but I think civilized people of all political persuasions recognize mean when we see it, whether we admit it or not. We're just more likely to call it mean if it's aimed at our side.

The odd thing is, when you meet him in the real world Misguided doesn't look like someone who should be locked away to keep society safe. But his Facebook posts make you think he has a secret life he's forgetting to keep secret.

I put up with Misguided's venomous drivel for a long time because, not being especially social media savvy, I was afraid he'd know if I unfriended him. Who knows? Maybe Mark Zuckerberg himself would send him a message saying, "Dorothy Rosby thinks you're a dolt, and she doesn't want to be your friend anymore," like a well-meaning friend would do for you in middle school.

But then one day, Misguided shared a doctored photo of a politician's family member that was as idiotic as it was cruel. His comment was, "Photos don't lie."

That did it. I started typing. "Photos do lie and so do you. Haven't you ever heard of Photoshop? Maybe you should try it on your picture. Even you could look intelligent with Photoshop."

Then I sat back, took a breath and deleted every word. And I'm glad I did. I see Misguided in the real world occasionally, and it might be awkward if I'd told him that he looks as witless as he apparently is.

I unfriended him instead, but only after determining that Facebook wouldn't tell him that I did it. Alas, he'll never know how I really feel unless I see him in public someday, lose my temper and throw a latte at him.

I won't have to deal with Misguided Fool during the next campaign season, but he's not the only wackadoodle out there. Unless I take a hiatus from Facebook, which I'm seriously considering, I'll have to deal with others like him. More importantly I'll have to deal with me.

Sometimes Facebook is like a giant coffee shop in cyberspace where people go to discuss and debate the issues of the day. More often it's just another battleground in the civil war that is a modern political campaign. Militaries have rules of engagement; in preparation for the upcoming battle, I've come up with mine.

1. I will do my part to stop the spread of Last Worditus, the highly contagious disease that starts when we see a post from someone who is deluded, misinformed and as wrong as a tuxedo with tennis shoes, and we're overcome with the urge to respond. I've been sucked in myself. I've attempted to make a witty, spontaneous response to someone's clearly

erroneous post, but it takes me a long time to sound witty and spontaneous. I carefully crafted my comment only to have her comment on my comment, apparently unconvinced. Also apparently faster at being witty and spontaneous than I am. Then I commented, she commented and days passed while I looked at my phone every few minutes to comment on her latest comment. And, it would have taken us both even longer if we'd bothered to check our facts before we posted. But who has time for that?

2.   And speaking of facts, I won't believe everything I read on Facebook even if I really want to believe it, and sometimes I really do want to. Before I hit share and muck up the newsfeeds of people I care about with some delicious tidbit about the checkered though possibly fictional past of a candidate, I'll go to Snopes.com or FactCheck.org to check it out. Or I'll do an internet search to determine if there are a variety of sources corroborating the sordid rumor. And then, even if it is true, I still may not share it. That's what cable news is for.

3.   I pledge to be respectful to all, even ding-a-lings, dimwits and anyone else I deem to be a few chads short of a full ballot. For one thing, I will never call them ding-a-lings and dimwits. I'll leave

the name calling to the candidates. This is not only polite, it's practical. I've never been persuaded to change my mind by someone who called me names so I imagine I'll never change anyone else's mind using that technique either, tempting as it may be.

4. I'll agree to disagree. I won't assume that just because I'm right, which most likely I am, that someone else is completely wrong even though they probably are.

5. I will never behave as badly as the people who I think behave badly. There's a race to the bottom on social media and while I normally don't do well in races, I think I could win this one if I chose to participate.

Two columnists I know, one from each side of the political aisle, have both told me that based on reader feedback the other side is clearly the rudest. I would have made the following insightful comment to each of them except I didn't think of it in time: Well, duh.

Of course the side that agrees with you is more polite—to you. They may not be so nice to someone they disagree with. If you doubt that, check out what they share on Facebook.

Great Waves
of Stupid

Elections bring out the worst in people, just like thunderstorms bring out earthworms and manure piles bring out flies.

To save you some heartache, I'm going to look into my crystal ball and tell you exactly what's going to happen between now and the next election. That way you can take a vacation from social media and cable news until it's all over but the voting.

First we'll have the candidates, some of whom think that just because they're opinionated they should be in charge. There are also plenty who are motivated by power, greed or a chance to see themselves on a billboard. But most are running for office because they sincerely want to make the world better. And I, for one, am grateful that someone wants the job.

Then we'll have the campaigns which will be as brutal as ever. Candidates will have access to the most expensive free speech money can buy, and how will they use it? They'll recount every mistake their opponent has made dating back to fifth grade, call them dim-witted evildoers or worse and then challenge them to run a positive campaign focusing on the issues.

And at the end of every ad, they'll say "I'm So-and-So and I approve of this message." And we'll think, "Really. You approve of that?" We would never talk about other people that way—at least not when they're within earshot.

Then there's us, the electorate, though "electorate" is a funny name to call us when the only electing many of us do is electing not to participate. I know you vote though. And I do. And we both mind our manners too. But as we near the election, plenty of people we know will behave as badly as the party they think behaves badly.

Facebook users will rant and rave and share stories so bizarre they could only come from tabloid journalists, Russian fiction writers or the other candidate's campaign staff.

Some of their friends will like what they post and some will unfriend them. And some will threaten to move to Canada if the other side wins, much to the pleasure of the other side and the dismay of the Canadians.

There will be polls and more polls. One side will point to them and say, "See. The American people love us." The other side will say, "We don't pay attention to polls." And when the polls switch, so will their opinions about polls.

One side will tune into Cable News Channel A and the other side will tune into Cable News Channel B just to reassure themselves they're still right about everything. Both sides will agree on one thing: There are some real wackadoodles out there. They just won't agree on who they are.

The pundits will blather on. Those who agree with them will think they should be canonized. Those who don't will think they should be cannon fodder.

There will be news and there will be fake news

and there will be much disagreement about which is which. There will also be talk shows that are almost as entertaining as sitcoms, but not nearly as enlightening. They will come in three formats:

Scenario One

A news show host looking for a fight will interview an individual he obviously disagrees with. You will be able to tell he disagrees because he will ask questions that are not really questions at all as much as they're opinions with question marks at the end. That's okay because he won't wait for an answer anyway. "Why did your candidate spill his coffee? Doesn't that say something about his potential as a leader?"

The interviewee, who also has a cantankerous streak, will try to respond. "Look here, you and I both know that there's no evidence to prove…."

The host, who has a better microphone and has watched too much court TV, will cut her off. "Now wait just a minute. You know this is not the first time Candidate X has been accused of this behavior."

The interviewee, who should have known better than to appear on this particular network, will say, "Yes, but…."

"The record clearly shows he also spilled his coffee in 2016 and twice in 2018. He has a history of this behavior."

"Yes, but...."

"Folks, the record clearly shows that Candidate X is untrustworthy. Thank you so much for joining me, you ignorant fool."

"Yes, but...."

If you want to hear the interviewee not only treated with respect but welcomed like a brilliant insightful hero, just switch networks, as we see in the following scene.

Scenario Two

A news show host will interview a person he obviously agrees with. You will be able to tell he agrees with the person because he will ask easy leading questions and won't interrupt when she answers. "Candidate X is taking some heat for spilling his coffee. He didn't do it, did he?"

"Absolutely not. In fact Candidate Y is the one who spilled coffee. Not only that, he failed to clean it up. The record shows that."

"Do you think Candidate Y is just bringing this up as strategy against Candidate X?"

"There's no question. Candidate Y is trying to draw attention away from his own coffee-spilling record. The American people expect better than that."

"They certainly do. Thank you for being with us and enlightening us on that very important point."

Scenario Three

The news show will welcome a group of experts who will yell at each other for the duration of the program. It will sound something like this:

"Blah, blah, blah."

"Yada, yada, yada."

"Wah, wah, wah."

When things get heated up, it will be more like, "Blah, yada, wah, yada, wah, blah."

You'll get the feeling the guests were invited based on their belligerence and that they're paid for each word they get into the conversation.

Watching all of this, you will be convinced that great waves of stupid are washing over this great land. But take heart. Eventually Election Day will arrive and not a moment too soon. If the campaign went on any longer, there would be a civil war.

Some people will vote; many will not. And in

the end, someone will win. I'm sorry my crystal ball doesn't tell me who, and after you read all this way. But it does tell me that billions of dollars will have been spent, enough to repair every road and bridge in the country, bring every school up to par and pay every politician's legal bills.

The two sides will finally agree on one thing. They're happy it's over—for now.

And no one will move to Canada, much to the relief of the Canadians. They've seen how we act during election years.

Campaign Tips for the Next President

So you want to run for president? What a coincidence! I want to be a campaign advisor and I have some sure-fire tips for a successful campaign.

First, have a lot of money. Better yet, have a lot of friends who have a lot of money. Votes aren't cheap these days, you know. (Neither are campaign advisors.)

And I don't care if you do have thirty years of leadership experience and a degree from Yale, don't even think about running for office if you don't do well on television. The average American watches more than four hours of television every day. By the time you show up on the evening news, you'd better be as media savvy as the anchor.

And this is no time to get chatty. Learn how to talk in sound bites. Ten seconds is about all the time you'll have to explain your resume, your plan for the future of this great nation and your opponent's many flaws. Remember, you're competing for air time with big newsmakers like Justin Bieber and Meghan Markle.

As a candidate, you'll have to make countless speeches. Here's a tip: Raising your voice's volume at the end of a sentence works as well as an applause sign. Compare: "We must cut the deficit," to "We must cut THE DEFICITTTTT!!!!!!!" Notice how this alerts the audience that it's time to clap and cheer even if they haven't been listening.

You'll want to sprinkle certain patriotic words throughout your speeches. Some examples include "freedom," "liberty" and "leadership." Useful phrases include "the American people deserve better" and "the American people want" this or that. Naturally, you'll only be referring to the American people who agree with you, but you don't have to say so.

The phrase, "Let me be very clear..." sounds especially presidential since candidates and presidents in trouble are the only ones who ever use it.

You'll want to use words like "inexperienced," "reckless," "foolish," "Washington insider" and "special interests" when you talk about your opponent. You'll also want to say you're deeply saddened by any scandals in his or her past and then go into detail about those. After all of this, it's a good strategy to challenge your opponent to run a clean campaign and stick to the issues.

Finish your speeches by telling everyone to get out there and vote. Of course, you really just want the people who'll vote for *you* to vote. The rest of them can all stay home and play Parcheesi as far as you're concerned. But don't ever say that.

Since you can't be everywhere at the same time, we'll plan on advertising a great deal. Political advertising comes in two varieties: boastful and mean.

To make a mean ad, we'll have to dig through all the photographs and video ever taken of the opposing candidate in search of the most unflattering ones. Maybe they sneezed just as the photo was taken or maybe it was taken at the end of a long day of campaigning, and a bit of five o'clock shadow is showing. This is especially effective if your opponent is a woman.

Then we'll sort through every interview and speech your opponent has given since eighth grade and choose short quotes that make them sound brainless or radical or both. An example might be, "I don't like Christmas." That will become the centerpiece of an ad used to draw all sorts of conclusions about your opponent's integrity, intelligence and patriotism even if the words were spoken in seventh grade after their hamster died on Christmas Day.

To be effective, a mean ad must feature the right voice. There are only two people voicing political commercials in this country today, one man and one woman. Okay, maybe there are more than two, but they all sound alike—pompous and sarcastic with just a touch of sincerity. They start their voice-over grimly. "The candidate who is not paying for this ad voted against world peace twelve times." Or "Candidate B says she supports apple pie, yet she voted against ala mode six times."

Then the music changes and the voice sounds pleased and self-satisfied as it says, "Whoever is paying for this rot supports Christmas, peace on earth and apple pie."

We'll want some shadowy organizations with names like "People for Happiness—at Least for Us" and "Citizens for Doing Things Our Way" to pay for the really mean ads. They're a little like the mob running Grandma's Diner; they sound wholesome on the face of it, but there's a lot going on in the backroom no one has to know about. One is reminded of the old saying, "He who pays the piper calls the tune." Or the modern version, "She who buys the band instrument ought to get to hear her kid play it." But that's another story.

Never fear. We'll have some positive ads too. These are the boastful ones. We'll show you at your best right after you've had your hair trimmed and your teeth whitened. You'll talk about how far you used to walk uphill to and from school every day and how, when you got home, you did your homework without being nagged and then worked in the family business until 2:00 or 3:00 in the morning.

You might even go out on a limb and say, "I'll cross the aisle to get things done." But don't be surprised if no one believes you'll be brave enough to do that. After all the nasty things you've said about the other party, it would take a whole lot of group therapy and some holding hands and singing

277

"Kumbaya" before they'd even say hello to you in the hallway.

It might be more effective if we just throw in something sweet, like you holding a small child or a puppy, to show your human side. This is good idea anyway since the ads we've been running about your opposition might have left voters wondering if you have one.

Go to Your Corners and Come out Voting

Just for kicks I'm going to suggest to my coworkers that we start working together the way our senators and representatives do. I don't think any of my team has actual experience serving in Congress, and if they do they're too embarrassed to admit it. But I still think we can pull it off because we were all children once.

We'll divide up based on which party we're registered in, and from then on, instead of our once cordial staff meetings, we'll meet separately to strategize—one side in the men's restroom and the other in the women's. We're a small department so we don't need a lot of space, plus the bathroom is a good metaphor for how things are going to be from here on out.

When we emerge from our secret bathroom meetings we won't want to talk to the other side, but we will want to talk *about* them. So we'll give a lot of media interviews where we'll take credit for anything good that's happening in the company and blame the other side for anything bad. We'll claim to be smart and principled and say that we alone have the best interests of our organization at heart. We'll say the other side is self-centered, incompetent and as uncooperative as a herd of drunken mules.

As much as we prefer to work with our own kind, eventually we'll have to come together, so just like in Congress and middle school, we'll only sit next to our friends and we'll vote with them no matter what the issue is. Sometimes this will be because we really believe it's the right way to vote, but most times it will be because that's how everyone else on our team is voting or because we're still mad at the other side for calling us drunken mules.

Unfortunately, we won't be able to vote based on

what our largest campaign donors want like they do in Congress. You have to campaign to get campaign donations, and we don't have that kind of time.

Sometimes we'll really want to make a point or just hold things up, so we'll stand up and pontificate for a while—a long while. We'll read out loud from Shakespeare or Dr. Seuss or the telephone book to fill the time. We'll blab and preach and carry on until the cows come home and then turn around and leave again because they can't take it anymore.

And like senators do, we might even tack unrelated riders onto whatever else we're voting on. For example, I plan to sneak in a rider calling for turning up the office thermostat because I don't see any other way to get everyone else to agree to it.

There you have it. From now on, this will be our mode of operation day after day, year after year. Go to your corner, come out fighting, then have recess. It will be fun.

Still, I suppose there will be times when even this system won't be quite dramatic enough for us. So now and then we'll have a dispute so serious that we'll shut down our business for a few days over it. This will be a great inconvenience to our customers and will cost our company a lot of money, but on the bright side we'll still get paid. On second thought, no, we probably won't.

Never mind.

CHAPTER SIX

Love Your Mother or She'll Kick Your...Behind

Big Foot Is Real and He's Living in My House

After a great deal of time and effort and some very careful calculations, I've managed to measure my carbon footprint. It turns out that much like my actual footprint, it's somewhere between a large and an extra large.

Actually, I didn't spend that much time nor did I calculate that carefully—or at all. I had good intentions though. Like a lot of people, I'm concerned about climate change. But I feel powerless to do much about it considering the current...uh...

climate, which I would describe as letting the house burn down while we all sit in the living room and argue about whether it's on fire or not.

So I was excited when I came across one of those online calculators used to determine how much greenhouse gas we're personally responsible for emitting into the atmosphere—in other words, how much of a gasbag each of us is. I was planning to write an insightful and informative essay on the subject, being well acquainted with many gasbags and having been called one myself on more than one occasion.

But once again, being insightful and informative proved to be too much for me, mainly because using the carbon footprint calculator would require a more organized filing system than I have. Among other things I'd need a year's worth of energy bills, an estimate of how many pounds of trash I recycle each year, the average miles per gallon each of our vehicles gets and an estimate of how many miles per week we drive them. Alternatively, I'd need someone else to figure it all out for me.

In the end I realized calculating my carbon footprint would take a lot more energy than I want to expend, especially since I'm trying to expend less energy. I don't know about you, but if your record keeping is anything like mine shrinking your footprint is probably easier than measuring it. And it's certainly less painful than shrinking your other footprint which as far as I know can only be done with drastic measures like cutting off your toes.

The bonus is that a smaller carbon footprint saves money, unlike with actual footprints where you pay the same for a size six and a size ten shoe, something I've always appreciated. So as a public service I'm providing the following tips for saving money while shrinking your carbon footprint. If you can't save the world, at least you can save some cash. And you get to keep your toes.

In the home there are many ways to shrink your family's carbon footprint besides the one we all think of first: Living in a cave without electricity and running water. Here are just a few:

- Slay your vampires, no wooden stake or garlic required. Vampire power, also known as standby power, refers to the electricity many gadgets and appliances waste just by being plugged in, even if they're switched off. It's like feeding a dead dog; it's wasteful and it doesn't do the dog any good anyway.

- Always turn off the lights when you leave a room. Be firm about this no matter how much it annoys those who are still in the room.

- Turn the thermostat down this winter. When family members complain, tell them to be quiet and go put on a coat. An angry person is a warm person.

- Remember a full freezer is more energy efficient than one that's partially full, so stock up on ice cream. Not only will this improve your freezer's efficiency, it will add to your own natural insulation.

- Don't waste food. A lot of energy goes into growing, packaging, shipping, refrigerating and cooking food. Tossing it into the landfill is like spending all your time planting, weeding and watering and then bulldozing your garden before you bring me any of your tomatoes.

Transportation is a major energy waster, but we

can't stay home all the time; we'd drive each other nuts. Instead, try these energy saving travel tips.

- Keep your vehicle in shape. Replacing your air filters regularly, keeping your tires properly inflated and having your radio properly tuned all help. Or maybe it's your engine. It's one of those.

- Slow down and not just because I hate it when you pass me. According to fueleconomy.gov, every five miles you go over fifty miles an hour is like paying an additional nineteen cents per gallon for gas. And that's on top of your speeding tickets.

- Combine errands to maximize fuel efficiency. Longer trips with a warm engine use half as much fuel as short ones, taken with a cold start, covering the same distance. Asking your neighbor to do your errands when they do theirs saves even more.

- Carpool whenever possible. I realize this may mean occasionally riding with people you don't particularly care for, and that can make the trip seem longer than it is. Try seeing them as large dollar signs—large dollar signs that talk too much.

- Avoid wasting gasoline by idling. For example, always choose the drive-through line that's moving the fastest. How will you know which line that is? Look for the line I'm in, then go to a different one. On the other hand, if you really want to idle, and who can blame you for that, don't do it with your engine running.

- Think about shopping for a more fuel-efficient vehicle, the most efficient being a bicycle.

- Don't fly if you can drive and don't drive if you can walk. Obviously you can't drive to New Zealand and, depending on where you live, you might not be able to walk to Cleveland either. But use your best judgment. Anyway, walking is good for your wallet, good for the earth and good for your health.

Or you could just stay home and lie on the couch which is also a great energy saver.

Useless
Stuff Day

Mark your calendar! The official start of the holiday season is the third Thursday of November when we celebrate Use Less Stuff Day, not to be confused with Useless Stuff Day which, for many of us, falls on December 25.

The average American throws away almost five pounds of trash every day. Use Less Stuff Day is a time for us to pause and ask ourselves the all-important question: If I had to haul my own garbage to the landfill, would I have so darn much of it?

And it rolls around just in time to remind us not to go overboard on the other major holidays we have coming up: Thanksgiving, Christmas, Black Friday and Cyber Monday. Between Thanksgiving and New Year's, we toss twenty-five percent more trash than we do the rest of the year. It's all that wrapping paper, packaging and fruitcake we haul to the curb, wrenching our backs and wrecking the holiday season for trash collectors everywhere.

What follows is my Christmas gift to you and all sanitation workers. It's not as much fun as a pet rock, but there's less packaging.

Six Ways to Use Less Stuff This Holiday Season

1. Clean up your Christmas card list. I read that there are more than two billion Christmas cards sold each year in the United States and that they'd fill a football field ten stories high. That would definitely interfere with the game.

I'd like to tell all my family and friends across the country that the reason I've all but stopped sending Christmas cards is out of concern for their landfills and their football stadiums, but that would be a lie.

The truth is I have good intentions, but good intentions do not send Christmas cards, at least not without assistance. On the bright side, my negligence has benefitted my community's landfill. Since I've stopped sending cards, no one sends me any either.

2. Make your own Christmas ornaments using items you already have on hand. Not only would you be recycling, but you could also make it a fun family project. But supervise closely. When my son was in kindergarten, he made an ornament by cutting his face out of his new 5x7 school portrait. He punched a hole through it and hung his creation on the tree with a bread bag tie. While I had to admire his ingenuity, that is not what I intended for the photograph I had just paid the equivalent of a year's worth of Christmas presents for.

3. Bring your own shopping bags. Americans use 100 billion plastic grocery bags every year. That's billion with a B. I'm trying to do my part. I use canvas bags, always remembering that the best canvas bag is the one you remember to bring to the store. I also reuse my plastic grocery bags over and over until the bottom falls out, which means occasionally I have to recycle a milk jug sooner than I intended.

4. Reuse ribbon and wrapping paper. Every

year, 38,000 miles of ribbon is used and discarded during the holiday season. That's enough ribbon to tie a bow around the earth though I'm not sure why we would do that.

I do reuse my holiday bows. I think the fact that they're usually squashed makes me look more organized by giving the impression that I purchased and wrapped the gifts months ago and have been storing them ever since.

I read that if we all wrapped just three presents in re-used materials rather than using new paper—it would save enough paper to cover 45,000 football fields. What a nice gift for the football fan in your life.

And remember, some gifts don't have to be wrapped at all, for example tickets, gift certificates and plants. I know I appreciate all of these. You could also just give me money.

5. Think outside the wrapped box. If you must wrap your gifts, you could make the wrapping part of the gift. For example, use a tea towel to wrap a package of kitchen sponges. Who wouldn't enjoy opening that?

You could also try wrapping your gifts in brown paper bags or old newspapers, being careful to avoid the obituary page.

I actually prefer using gift bags myself. They're attractive. They're sturdy, so they can be used over and over. And they make it easy for me to peek.

6. Don't buy dumb gifts. More knickknacks, gimcracks, doohickeys and thingamajigs are purchased just before Christmas than any other time of the year, many of them in those last frantic moments before the reindeer appear. Shoppers who started out with great intentions break down on December 24 and settle for an electric carrot peeler. Not only does the package end up in the landfill, so does the gift. You have options:

- **Give your time instead of buying physical gifts.** Volunteer to babysit or help a friend with home improvement projects. If I'm on your gift list—and I sincerely hope I am— you could just come clean my gutters.

- **Give a donation to a favorite charity in your friend or family member's name.** Young children are especially fond of this gift.

- **Make gifts yourself.** Weave a rug out of some

of your extra plastic bags or give away the homemade Christmas ornaments that didn't turn out so well. I'm joking. Homemade gifts really can be wonderful. But if you're planning to give me a fruit basket made with Popsicle sticks, I'd rather have the Popsicles.

- **Remember that old saying, it's better to regift than to receive.** Some people may be offended to learn their gift is a regift so make sure you don't give a gift back to the person who gave it to you in the first place.

  If someone on your gift list finds out you've regifted something to them, tell them that you liked the gift so much that you thought they might like one of their own.

  Or you could be honest. Tell them gently that you felt it was better to regift than to add the item to the nearly five pounds of trash you're already throwing away every day. That should make them feel better.

Seeking Long-Term Relationships

A co-worker once asked me if I grew up during the Depression. "No, I did not," I snapped. "But at least I grew up."

I might have been a little defensive, but she was teasing me about my ancient radio and she wasn't the first person to do it. The radio was a hand-me-down from my husband who bought it before we met, and we met a long time ago. He was going to toss it, so I rescued it and took it to my office because it still worked—usually.

Sometimes it didn't come on when I turned it on. And sometimes it came on when I didn't turn it on. It was like magic, but that's not why I kept it.

I didn't keep it for sentimental reasons either. When it quit working altogether I disposed of it and took my son's castoff boom box to my office, and it's been there ever since.

And I didn't keep the radio because I'm too cheap to buy a new one. I'm not cheap. I might not even qualify as thrifty. I rarely shop sales and I eat avocados—a lot. Nobody who buys as many avocados as I do could be called thrifty. Those things are green because they're made of money. The only reason I can afford them is because I've saved so much on radios.

I've saved a lot not replacing other things too. My bathrobe and my sheepskin bedroom slippers are both at least twenty years old. They're still in good shape though—at least by my standards, which may not be that high if my radio is any indication.

The travel case I used for more than thirty years to carry my toothbrush and travel shampoo wasn't in good shape by anybody's standards. Looking at it, you'd think I travel a lot more than I do. But it still did the job so I used it until my sister, who travels with me occasionally, got tired of looking at it and gave me a new one. I love it! It's got a place for everything. It's purple and it's obviously well made. I bet it lasts longer than the old one did.

So yes, I save money keeping things until they disintegrate or someone else replaces them for me but that's not why I do it either.

Forgive me now while I talk some trash. I once toured the material recovery facility in my community. At some point during the tour, I stood in a huge room where the garbage trucks drop their loads daily. There were literally mountains of garbage. It looked like New Year's Day at Time's Square only more organized. It was shocking and smelly and I didn't throw anything away for a month. I couldn't keep that up though, or my house would be shocking and smelly too.

But it did make me aware of how much I throw away. Americans generate 4.7 pounds of garbage per person every day. Less than a quarter of it is recycled; the rest is incinerated or buried in landfills. How nice of us. We dig up raw materials from Mother Earth then return them to her as trash. It's like borrowing our mother's car then dragging it back to her with a tow truck.

Keeping my radio, bathrobe and slippers for as long as I can seems like the least I can do. I appreciate durable products. That explains the giant ancient radio and it explains my old reliable laptop. It weighs more than my new desktop computer and probably more than the desk it sits on. But it keeps on working. There are times when I'm hauling it through an airport that I wish it would quit—but not until I get it home.

Durability is a touchy subject for me right now because my dishwasher has started leaving food behind. That means I have to wash the dishes before it washes the dishes or risk having to wash them after it washes them. That's much harder because the heat-dry part of the cycle works fine.

I'm not sure how old my dishwasher is, but I do know it's still sticky where the price tag used to be. Or maybe that's not why it's sticky. At any rate, I've had avocados that lasted longer.

When I find something that holds up—be it a bathrobe, a laptop or a radio—I keep it because so many things don't hold up. With the exception of my bathrobe and slippers everything in my house is practically new. Well, almost everything. My stove, computer, printer, vacuum cleaner and garage door opener are all just a few years old. No, I didn't win big on *The Price is Right.* Everything in my house is nearly new because a short time ago it all quit working at the same time.

If you know me well, you might be saying, "Hey, wait! Didn't your oven quit working a long time ago?" Yes it did, which is why for years I hinted to you and everyone else I know that a new stove would make a great birthday or Christmas gift. Nobody listens to me.

I continued to use my old unreliable oven because at one point a repairman told me if I added thirty degrees to whatever temperature setting the recipe called for, I could get by for a long time, especially as little as I use my oven.

Then one year, shortly before Thanksgiving, adding thirty degrees didn't work anymore. Adding fifty degrees didn't work either. I threw away a pan of half-baked cookies and went shopping. There were only a few stoves in stock that would work for us. But I decided buying a new stove just because it was in stock and I needed to make Thanksgiving dinner in two days might be hasty, especially since I didn't want to cook Thanksgiving dinner anyway. (I know what you're thinking. What could be hasty about taking years to replace an oven?)

One issue was color. I'm no designer but I wanted my new stove to match my ancient refrigerator, one of the few things in my home that was still working. But appliance manufacturers no longer make anything in harvest gold. I'm joking. My refrigerator isn't harvest gold; it's almond. But compared to today's models, it's a clearly from a different batch of almonds.

The appliance industry updates colors regularly so that when you buy a new stove, you feel compelled to buy a refrigerator, dishwasher, microwave, washer, dryer and a pair of shoes to match. It seems to me if you buy all that, they ought to give you the microwave—and the shoes.

I didn't want to replace all my appliances, but I did ask if, since we were buying a stove, would they throw in a vacuum cleaner for free? Ours had died recently, and I didn't care if the new one matched. No, they would not. "Okay," I said, "If we buy a vacuum cleaner and computer, would you throw in a stove?" It never hurts to ask.

And we did need a computer. Our desktop had started dozing off at inopportune times—much like I do.

Just when I thought I couldn't take another thing, our humidifier started wetting on the carpet and my garage door opener developed a bad attitude. Sometimes it worked and sometimes it didn't—meaning sometimes I could get into my garage and sometimes I had to call someone in the house to come open the door for me. It's hard to say which of us found that most annoying.

There we were, with everything falling apart around us like a beach house in a hurricane. We replaced the computer first, as most important. We followed with the vacuum cleaner, the garage door opener, the humidifier and finally, after years of adding thirty degrees to everything I put in the oven, we bought a new stove. It's a hard habit to break—I set off the smoke alarm every time I use it.

After several very expensive months, we'd managed to replace everything, ensuring that eventually it will all quit working again at exactly the same time. And we had barely learned how to use it all when, wouldn't you know it, my printer stopped printing, which, as far as I can tell, is the only thing a printer is good for, even one with brand new cartridges.

Yes, it's true. I had just replaced them. New

printers are cheap; ink is not. Buying a new printer is like getting a free membership into the elite Cyan, Magenta and Yellow Club and not being able to afford the monthly dues. If my printer were a car, I'd have to leave it parked in the garage because I couldn't afford the gas. But what can I do? A printer without ink is nothing more than a place to stack paperwork and I've already got plenty of those.

But this is not a rant about printer ink, though I could probably carry on about that for a page or two. If you haven't figured it out by now—and I wouldn't blame you if you haven't—this is a rant about how fast stuff falls apart and not only my stuff either.

Even I, who keeps things until death do we part, am finding we're parting faster. And I'm not the only one who thinks so. Appliances really don't last as long as they used to. I read it on the internet so it must be true. I'm not sure about electronics because they're obsolete long before they quit working—and sometimes before I've figured out how to use them.

And do you know who's to blame? You are! And I am. And so is everyone else who cares more about cost and the latest trend than quality. At least that's who manufacturers like to blame. They claim that manufacturing costs continue to go up, but consumers want cheap products. Wouldn't we spend less in the long run if we bought one high-priced appliance that lasted thirty years than if we bought a less expensive one every ten years? Naturally it would be out of style after five. That's the problem. We want everything: style, affordability and durability. Affordable ink would be nice too.

Which brings me back to my old bathrobe. It's affordable—I already own it. It's clearly durable. Plus it's stylish—or it was twenty years ago. And I'm loyal. If I have to replace my dishwasher, I will have loaded and unloaded four dishwashers while wearing this bathrobe—not to mention cursed a host of other appliances and electronics. Is it any wonder I've kept it? We've been through a lot together.

Leave Recyclables
to Grandchildren

I admit it. I reuse plastic cutlery. Don't worry; I wash it first. And it's not like I'm reusing paper plates. "Disposable" just seems like a funny way to describe something that will outlast us, our children, grandchildren, great grandchildren and probably their stainless steel knives, forks and spoons too. Heck, we could pass down plastic cutlery as family heirlooms. "See this fork, honey? Your great grandmother ate cake with it at her fourth birthday party."

Besides, spending money on something so

durable and using it only once feels wasteful to someone who grew up wearing darned socks.

I know some people prefer we not reuse plastic cutlery—the makers of plastic cutlery for example. And some people find it distasteful to eat with a plastic spoon someone else ate with first, so I don't tell them.

Still others say if you're going to reuse plastic cutlery, why not just use the real thing in the first place? My thoughts exactly. It turns out there's a whole month set aside for people like us. Welcome to Plastic Free July!

Plastic Free July began in Australia in 2011 to raise awareness about the problems of single-use disposable plastic and to challenge us to do something about it. I was trying to do something about it long before I heard about Plastic Free July. For years I've carried a giant reusable mug with me wherever I go. I drink water out of it. I drink iced tea and diet cola out of it. The only beverages I don't drink out of it are milk, juice and whiskey—because then I'd have to wash it more often. Plus I don't care for whiskey.

I've even been known to rummage through other people's trash, take out their plastic bottles and put them in the recycling bin. They don't appreciate it as much as you'd think they would.

Millions of people from around the world now participate in Plastic Free July by pledging to avoid buying single-use plastic items for the month. If I can convince everyone I know to join us, I won't have to dig through anyone's trash for thirty-one whole days. I would love that. They probably would too.

Obviously Plastic Free July is just the beginning. We won't make much headway if, come August, we stock up on bottled water and plastic forks. And single-use plastic is hard to avoid. My detergent, shampoo and dishwashing soap all come in plastic bottles. I dream of a day when stores are filled with giant barrels of shampoo and lotion. You'll walk in with your empty bottle and say, "fill 'er up." But for now people like me will keep washing plastic spoons and digging through everyone else's trash looking for plastic bottles.

And we'll find them. Americans throw away fifty million plastic beverage bottles every day. Honestly, I don't see how we get anything else done.

And I'm not convinced some bottled water isn't just a scam anyway. There are hundreds of brands of bottled water with pretty names like Something Springs, Fresh This and Aqua That. I wonder if some of them should be called Pure Bologna. I picture employees filling bottles from a faucet then sticking on pretty labels with pictures of waterfalls on them.

Just to be clear, I don't take plastic forks out of anyone's trash—or Styrofoam cups and straws. I may be concerned but I'm not crazy. Also, those aren't recyclable.

I wish they were. Americans toss twenty-five billion Styrofoam cups every year which is a whole lot of hot chocolate and coffee. The number of straws we discard is not as clear, though maybe we could make an educated guess if we all started digging them out of the other people's trash.

And don't get me started on plastic bags. Oh, too late. Up to a trillion plastic bags are used worldwide each year, but less than one percent are recycled. And do you know where the other ninety-nine percent go? Into my yard, that's where.

I'm exaggerating. But I'm a little touchy about the subject right now because there's been a plastic bag tangled in the cottonwood tree outside my dining room window for more than six months. Based on my research on plastic, there's a good chance it will outlast the tree.

And plastic isn't the only issue. Take a close look at that aluminum can the next time you have a pop—or a soda or a soda pop, depending on where you are when you're drinking it. I hope you like it because, according to my good friend Google, that aluminum can will still be around for the next 200 to 400 years unless you recycle it. Your food cans will last around fifty years though I don't think you should wait that long to eat your tuna and green beans.

It's sobering to think that our great great grandchildren won't even know who we are, but they could still be kicking our cans—and bottles—down the driveway. That's why I've decided to leave my descendants aluminum cans and plastic forks instead of money. They'll last longer. And I have more of them.

Business is
Picking Up

Early one morning I cleaned up what remained of someone's supper off a picnic table at the park. Then I picked up a gum wrapper, a beer can, a Styrofoam cup and a five-foot long grocery receipt. But when I noticed that someone had hauled in a beat-up recliner and left it at the baseball field, I couldn't take it anymore. I'd had it with picking up other people's trash. And not just because I couldn't lift the recliner.

I was out for a walk. This was supposed to be

my happy time and it was being spoiled by other people's bad manners so I quit. Just like that. I walked by a fast food bag without slowing down. I hurried past an aluminum can and a half-empty plastic bottle. I was in no mood to consider it half full.

But then I spotted an empty plastic grocery bag. I couldn't help myself. I picked it up and filled it with trash by the time I got home.

You wouldn't come into my house and leave litter all over my living room, would you? Of course not. Only my immediate family does that.

Everyone knows that kind of behavior is unacceptable. So why would anyone think it's okay to leave garbage laying around outdoors? What are they thinking? "Leave it. Someone will pick it up." You're darn tootin' someone will pick it up, and that someone is me. For reasons I can't explain, I feel compelled to pick up litter when I see it. It's odd really, because I don't always feel the need to pick it up in my own home.

But I don't pick up trash cheerfully. I mutter and grumble and curse litterers. "What? Were you born in a dumpster? Raised in a landfill?"

You may not be aware of this but the reason people who litter are called litterbugs is because they bug me. Okay, maybe that's not the reason. But they do bug me. Litter eventually ends up in waterways, tangling up critters or being eaten by poor unsuspecting fish who mistake candy wrappers for actual candy. It makes road ditches and parks look like an episode of *Hoarders*. And it attracts critters no one wants hanging around, like flies, rats and bad-tempered walkers like me.

Frankly I think there should be harsher penalties for litterers. Along with a stiff fine and public humiliation, they should be sentenced to accompany me on a walk. I'd supervise as they picked up every plastic cup, every beer can and every dirty diaper in our path. Worse, they'd be subjected to my ranting. And if you've read this far, you know how I can rant.

Just how well I can carry on about littering was made clear to me once when my son was very young. He'd already misplaced plenty of items in his short life but I'd never seen him as upset over losing something as he did when the wind apparently took a picture he'd taped to the outside of our house. I told him to go out into the yard and look as far as he could see in every direction. "I looked everywhere," he said when he came back in. "I can't find it." And he started to cry.

I thought this seemed a little dramatic until he asked me if he would be "under arrested" for littering. Ah ha.

While I'm sure I never actually told him that people who litter are arrested, I probably did tell him they should be. And I remember exactly when I said it. (One of the times anyway.) He and I had taken a walk on the hill behind our home. We were having a wonderful time until we came across a pile of broken beer bottles, empty cigarette packages and pages torn from adult magazines.

Somewhere in the tirade that followed I may or may not have said that those responsible should go to jail for the rest of their sorry lives and that after they die, they should spend all eternity picking up trash. Or something like that.

I've got to come clean here, so to speak. I've littered a few times myself, but I swear it was an accident and I've always gone to great lengths to pick up after myself. I once chased an empty tin can all the way down the hill by my house, and I live on a big hill. If I had tripped, I'd still be rolling.

One time I littered during a girl's day out with a friend. My fingernails were still wet with polish after my first and only manicure. I pushed the door of the salon open with my hip and walked across the parking lot with my hands up and my fingers splayed. I looked like I was being robbed. As I gingerly opened the door, a gust of wind swept a paper off the floorboards and out the door of my friend's car. I thought it might be something important, like the deed to her house, so I chased it across the parking lot and retrieved it from behind the wheel of a parked car. Then I surveyed the damage: Two scraped nails and a tread mark up my arm—and all to save a furniture store flyer. My friend said that while she appreciated the effort, she normally doesn't keep the deed to her house on her floorboards.

Another time I wasn't so successful. As I got out of my car, a gust of wind blew a paper off my dashboard onto the parking lot and under my car. I closed the door and set my purse, briefcase and giant jug of iced tea on the ground while I reached under my car for the paper. That's when I realized that my car was still running and that at some point, I'd apparently locked my doors. Uh-oh. Fortunately I keep a spare key in my purse. As I reached for the key I knocked over my drink, and a puddle formed under me and my belongings. My knees were muddy. My purse and briefcase were wet. My iced tea was gone.

My car was running with the doors locked. And the paper that had started it all was airborne again and on its way to somebody else's parking lot. It's all right though. I'm sure I picked it up the next time I was in the neighborhood.

Save Water. Shower
with a Friend.

I leave my house in the dawn's early light wearing only my SpongeBob jammies and my bedroom slippers. It's a beautiful morning. The birds are just starting to sing, but I'm not enjoying it. My neighbor's sprinkler system is chirping too. His lawn looks like a forest green shag carpet. Mine looks like matted dog hair.

My sprinkler system doesn't chirp. My sprinkler system is a hundred feet of hose and a rotating, pulsating gizmo we bought at a garage sale a few years back. And I would rather pour green concrete all over my lawn then haul it around my yard. But haul it I must—if I can find it. I wander across my crunchy lawn peering into the dim light. Where did I water last? When did I water last? Are lawns supposed to crunch?

Mine does. Maybe that's because weeks go by with no water from me. Then one day I notice that my grass is looking ill. By this time it's a matter of choosing which brown spot is the brownest and watering that first. So many brown spots, so little time. For me lawn watering is an endless act of triage.

It's still too dark to tell which spots are brownest, but there are so many of them lately it shouldn't be hard to hit one wherever I plant the sprinkler. I decide to start in front of the house. At least I'll look like a responsible homeowner from the street.

I trip over the hose, pick myself up and follow it to the sprinkler. I drag the hose across the yard feeling like a draft horse while the neighbor's sprinkler system ticks away in the background. He can't possibly have the upper body strength I have—or would have if I watered as often as I should.

I make a wide swath on the lawn until—what? I'm out of hose? How can that be? Oh, I see. I'll have to backtrack around that cottonwood tree. Dang. Did I just take the heads off those tiger lilies?

I finally pick a spot in the front yard, carefully place the sprinkler and go to the faucet to turn it on. I'll be darned. I've set it perfectly—to water the driveway.

I wait. I watch. Then I dash for the sprinkler at the exact moment it's spraying away from me. At least, it was spraying away from me when I started running.

I pick up the sprinkler and wrestle it back and forth in an effort to get more water on my lawn and less on the driveway—and me. I'm glad no one else is up. From a distance I bet I look like I'm wrestling with a wet wildcat, and it's winning.

I finally get the sprinkler lined up and quickly back away. My backside is still dry and I'd like to keep it that way. Just then someone says, "Good morning." I jump and turn to see Mr. Sprinkler System standing on his front step with his newspaper. Mine is lying in wet heap on my driveway.

I'm about to draw attention away from my PJs with a witty remark about squandering precious moisture on a vain wasteful luxury. Instead I let out a little yelp as the sprinkler squanders more of it down my back.

I curse my neighbor under my breath. May his sprinkler system break down and flood his basement. Then I head to the house to take a shower which now seems redundant.

Moments later I'm standing under the warm spray praying for rain and forgiveness and wondering why I ever chose to live next door to a guy with a lawn that looks like a golf course. The grass really is greener on the other side of the fence. I just wish my neighbors could say that.

Oh, who cares? Lawns are dumb anyway. They're attractive but high maintenance, pretty but senseless—the bimbos of landscaping. After spending so much time hauling hoses around my lawn, I can't help but wonder if there isn't a better use of my time and water. And if maybe it's not the lawn that's so dumb.

I like my lawn for about half a day every spring. It turns green and asks little of me. But as the days wear on it gets more and more needy. There's bindweed and crabgrass and the dandelions pop up like spam in my inbox.

And since we hired someone to fertilize the grass and kill the weeds the lawn looks worse. At least the weeds were green. Without them there's nothing covering the bald spots. Between cuttings our grass is Mother Nature's version of a comb over. And that seems like a very good reason not to mow. Not that I do.

My husband does that. I rake, pull weeds and water now and then but I do not mow. That's because part of our lawn is on a very steep hill and I'm not as tough as I look. I'd be risking my life mowing the hill. I let my husband risk his instead. Neglecting to water is one small kindness I can show him. Plus I'm hoping he'll water if I don't.

You may be thinking that if we'd water more, we wouldn't have so many bare spots, and you'd be right. But you haven't seen our lawn. It's big, and as the summer wears on it gets bigger. Honest. In the spring it's the size of a football field. At least it seems that way. By fall it's as big as an eighteen-hole golf course with extra hazards. If you think I'm exaggerating, come over and drag hoses around it for a while.

In fact, I'd like that very much. We could use the help. It would take an in-ground sprinkler system or a truly dedicated waterer to keep our gigantic lawn green. There's no sprinkler system in my future and no dedicated waterers in my house.

That's one reason that, while I do not enjoy drought, I don't mind at all the accompanying water restrictions. Fact is, as long as I can take a shower, water restrictions don't affect me at all.

At least when there are water restrictions, pass-ersby assume my lawn looks the way it does because of the restrictions. Another positive of water restrictions is that if they continue long enough, my neighbor's lawn will start looking more like mine. And if it doesn't, I'll know he's cheating.

All the talk of water and conserving it brings back memories of my father who died just after I graduated from college. He was the Water and Sewer Superintendent for my hometown. It was a fancy title for an important job in a town of few people, little water and no sprinkler systems, at least that I was aware of. Along with the many other things my father did (plowing snow, driving ambulance, fighting fire) he saw to it that everybody had plenty of clean water.

And water runs through the memories I have of my father. But "runs" is the wrong word. He would never have let the water run unless it was for a very good reason. And I'm not saying how I know this, but he didn't consider stirring up a batch of mud in the bottom of the shower a very good reason.

My father believed in conserving water maybe because he was well aware of how little of it we had. My siblings and I were amused and amazed that our usually proper father had a button stuck to his office wall that read, "Save water. Shower with a friend."

I once won many points with my dad because I crawled out of bed late one night and went downstairs to make sure I'd turned the water off in the bathroom. Most people would see that for what it was: the beginning of a future of compulsive behavior. But my dad was proud. He saw it as a sign that I would grow up to conserve water.

And he was right. Growing up in an area so susceptible to drought with the father I had helped form my philosophy of water use, which can basically be put this way: Water restrictions or not, you should live as though you have to pump your own water and carry it up the hill. For example, if I had to carry my own water would I do laundry? Yes, but no more often than I had to. If I had to carry my water would I wash dishes? Absolutely not. I'd eat out. If I had to pump my own water and carry it up the hill would I water my lawn? Are you kidding? I can't even bring myself to drag a hose around my yard.

What's it all for anyway? After a summer of plucking weeds, dragging hoses and watching my husband mow, I'm rewarded with a ton of cotton-wood leaves and pine needles to rake in the fall. Both are deadly to grass. It's reminds me of a Liam Neeson movie. "Rake or the lawn dies."

Unfortunately there are no truly dedicated rakers in our house either. Our lawn doesn't stand a chance between the leaves and the pine needles—and me.

But this morning while I was dragging the hose across my lawn, I stopped and looked up at the hills behind my house. No one waters, rakes or mows them, but they're beautiful. That's when it hit me. Crabgrass and dandelions are not the problem. Hoses are not the problem. Cottonwood leaves and pine needles are not the problem. The lawn is the problem. That and a shortage of dedicated rakers and waterers.

The Food Chain
Ticks On

I picked up a hitchhiker on a recent trip. I gave him a ride and a good meal, then I squashed him and flushed him down the toilet. I bet you'll never ask me for a ride. Relax. You'd have done the same thing. The hitchhiker was a tick which, not coincidentally, rhymes with "ick."

I know there's a big old food chain out there. I know that everything on the planet has a role whether we understand it or not. I know that God don't make no junk. But ticks? Really? And flies and mosquitoes? (I bet God don't use no double negatives either, but that's a topic for another day.)

Let's define our terms here. There are insects and there are arachnids. Insects have six legs, three main body parts and usually, though not always, wings. Ticks aren't insects; they're arachnids which have two body segments, eight legs and no wings. In other words we get it from all sides: arachnids by land, insects by air.

If I sound like I know what I'm talking about, it's only because I went to the internet to research how ticks tick. I've always called the whole mess of them bugs because they bug me. And I'll probably still call them that even now that I know better because I don't feel like counting legs every time I see one.

But I do have a grudging admiration for all of them. Fleas can flee, flies can fly and butterflies can flutter by. Crickets can crick and bees can buzz and mosquitos can find their way back home after picking up carryout—from me.

Ticks are talented too. They can sit all day on a blade of grass with their little front legs waving in the air until another critter passes by and brushes against them. Then they climb on and start looking for lunch. It can mean going days without food. I could never do that. That's like waiting to ambush a pizza delivery guy without placing an order.

And of course all bugs perform vital functions in our ecosystem. They pollinate plants. They aerate and fertilize the soil. I'm not sure why they keep coming into my house. Contrary to what you might think, I don't have that much soil.

But I do appreciate their role as food for birds, reptiles, fish and other critters because I don't want to have to feed them all myself. The problem is that bugs have to eat too, and that's where I draw the line. At the very least, bug bites cause itching and pain. At their worse they spread disease to their hosts which seems like a wicked thing to do to someone who has just given you a good meal.

Not to oversimplify but the food chain can be summed up by that classic song that begins, "I know an old woman who swallowed a fly, but I don't know why she swallowed that fly. I guess she'll die." After swallowing the fly, she swallowed a spider, a bird, a cat, a dog, a goat, a cow and finally a horse all in a vain attempt to catch the unfortunate critter that had gone before.

This song has much to teach us: Don't bite off more than you can chew. Keep your mouth closed when there are flies around. Every organism has to eat, and some not only have to eat, they have to be eaten in order for creatures higher up the food chain to eat—me, for example. It all works fine and dandy—unless you're the one being eaten.

I may be stretching things a bit since cows and horses are vegetarians. And if the old woman had known that, she might still be with us today. Nevertheless I think the song does make an interesting point about the food chain. I know it. I respect it. I just don't think it has to happen in my basement.

Every fall the spiders and flies and everyone else involved in the food chain start moving into my warm house. Well, not everyone. No birds, goats or horses yet. But we once had a beetle in our basement that was so big I suspect it stood up on its hind legs and let itself in the front door. My son had mercy on it and took it outside because that's what he would have done if a mammal that size had wandered into our house.

In some cultures a cricket in the home is a sign of good luck, but I know that doesn't hold true in our culture because I've had way more crickets in my house than I've had good luck. So when I heard one under my desk one morning, I got on my knees to track it down like the criminal that it was. I planned to charge it with breaking and entering and disturbing the peace.

I couldn't see the cricket, but I could see a huge spider, probably on its way to find the cricket. I think it was a wolf spider because it was about the size of a wolf. In retrospect I wish I'd let the spider find the cricket. Then I could have taken care of them both at the same time. But I killed the spider and spent the rest of the morning listening to the cricket sing, probably a happy little ditty about being spared from the big bad wolf...spider.

A few years ago, our home was on the migration path for some type of moth. They were everywhere. The birds loved it. They were so fat and happy they could barely lift off the ground. I couldn't lift off the ground either, but I wasn't as happy. My biggest concern was that the moths in my house wouldn't hear the news when it was time to travel on.

Every time I turned on a light, I felt like I should apologize. "I'm sorry! Am I disturbing you?" They flew out of my newspaper. They flew around inside my car when I was driving. One even flew out of my dishwasher. Fortunately the dishwasher hadn't been run yet. I don't know what I would have done if the moth had come out washed, rinsed and sanitized.

Through it all that song kept going through my head. I know an old woman who swallowed a fly, but I don't know why she didn't have a fly swatter. She could have prevented the whole mess.

Yes, bugs tick me off. (I've been dying to say that.) I've found black widow spiders in my garage. I've been stung by wasps. I've seen bugs the size of full-grown Chihuahuas in my basement. And it turns out the hitchhiker that started this rant had a partner. I found it a few days later in my laundry basket and I don't think it was planning to help with the laundry either.

Still I understand bugs do important work so I'll try to maintain my uneasy truce with them. As long as they stay away from me I'll let them go about their business. In his book *The Diversity of Life*, biologist Edward O. Wilson says that if all insects disappeared, amphibians, reptiles, birds and mammals would soon follow because of the domino effect on up the food chain. I did not read Mr. Wilson's book and I probably never will but I do take his warning seriously. I like the food chain just the way it is.

Are You Going to Eat That?

There's a turkey the size of Plymouth Rock thawing in my refrigerator when I stumble across the following startling statistic on the internet: Americans throw away nearly a pound of food every day. I go to my refrigerator, open the door and stare at my colossal turkey. I'll be serving six for Thanksgiving and that includes me and my cat. Maybe I should give the turkey to someone with a longer guest list and roast a package of hotdogs instead. Nah. They don't go as well with cranberries.

But I could do more to stop food waste. I read somewhere else that average Americans throw away about twenty-five percent of the food and beverages they purchase. That's like going the grocery story, buying four bags of food and beverages then putting one in the trashcan as you're leaving the store. I believe if I put a little effort into it, cutting back on food waste will be one more area of my life where I'm below average.

According to my research, reducing food waste comes down to four simple steps.

1) Plan menus. Menu planning should be easier for me than it is because I cook the same five meals over and over. The problem is, there are days when I just can't face them one more time. Fortunately, I have an entire drawer stuffed with recipes clipped from magazines. I call it my Dream Drawer because I dream that someday someone will come into my home and cook them for me.

I also have more cookbooks than Rachael Ray. I have so many cookbooks that the shelf in my kitchen cupboard is bowed from the weight of them all, but don't take that as a sign that I like to cook. Most of them were gifts from people who were hoping I'd make something new for our next potluck.

Looking at cookbooks is almost always a mistake. As I gaze at the beautiful food photographs I'm overcome by optimism. I convince myself that not only will I have time to brine a pork roast or stuff chicken breasts with a mixture of chopped mushrooms, spinach and feta cheese, I'll feel like doing it when the time comes.

I may even go so far as to pick up the ingredients for the Marrakesh Vegetable Curry or the Walnut Crusted Blue Cheese Potato Cakes. But then I come home tired and hungry. So we eat grilled cheese sandwiches and tomato soup from a can, and the ingredients for the curry and the potato cakes are forgotten in my refrigerator. You may not realize this, but eventually even blue cheese can go bad.

I plan to start planning, but if I'm going to stop food waste in my home as I'm determined to do, I may need to stick to my simpler cookbooks, like the *It's Fun to Cook* cookbook that my mother gave me when I was eleven.

2) Make a grocery list. None of the articles I read on the subject of reducing food waste mentioned this, but I know from experience that the best grocery list is the one you remember to bring to the store. That saves you from having to rely on memory which, in my case is notoriously unreliable, witness the fact that I keep forgetting to bring my list to the store.

Many times I've come home tired and hungry, planning to make something quick like spaghetti with meat sauce and a tossed salad, then realized I'd forgotten to buy one of the ingredients—like spaghetti.

Also, a grocery list is only as good as your willingness to follow it. There are two reasons I go off script at the grocery store. One is that I'm a sucker for BOGO. I once had two ten-pound bags of Russet potatoes rotting in my basement because I'm willing to spend twice as much for an item that's advertised as "Buy one get one free."

The second reason I purchase items that aren't on my list is because…well…I want them. (Some examples include chocolate, chocolate and chocolate.) Fortunately when I buy something I love that's not on my list it seldom winds up in the trash. Sometimes it doesn't even make it to my car.

3) Store food in a safe and organized manner. Disorganization makes it harder to remember what you have. You go about your life oblivious to the fact that somewhere in the depths of your refrigerator expiration dates are passing and perishables are perishing.

Not only that, it's costly. I keep buying things I already have because I don't know I have them. That explains why I have two fourteen-ounce containers of mustard. The label says fourteen ounces equals seventy-nine servings. That's 158 servings of mustard in a home where there are no hot dogs—that I know of.

4) Eat your leftovers, or at least force your family to eat them. When it comes to reducing food waste, this is the one area where I excel though my family may not see it as a talent.

I can almost guarantee none of our turkey is going into the trash. When I look at that giant bird thawing in my refrigerator I don't just see Thanksgiving dinner, I see turkey soup, turkey sandwiches, turkey casserole, turkey ala king, turkey hash, turkey enchiladas, turkey tetrazzini, turkey this and turkey that for weeks to come. I'm starting to wonder if my turkey is big enough.

Eating leftovers is not just a great way to keep food out of the landfill. It has a lot of other benefits as well.

- Not only do you spend less time planning meals, grocery shopping, cooking and washing pots and pans, your family doesn't waste nearly as much time eating.

- The family stays slim and trim. Forget the low-carbohydrate and low-fat diets. Try the leftover food diet. After eight or nine days of leftover turkey, I guarantee your appetite will be depressed. I mean suppressed.

- Serving leftovers saves money which you can spend eating out.

- Unwelcome guests rarely return, and if they do they bring food.

- And it really is true what some people say: Certain foods are actually better the second time they're served. Careful observation will reveal the people who say this are usually the people who cooked them.

Those of us who are unencumbered by good taste regularly enjoy these benefits of serving leftovers. I don't mean to brag, but if I buy enough freezer paper I can not only keep our turkey out of the landfill, I can freeze enough leftovers to last through the Fourth of July. Now there's something to be thankful for.

Hand Over
Your Chocolate

Early one morning I opened my internet newsfeed to the following shocking headline: "The Earth Is Running Out of Chocolate." That's no way to start a day if you're me. But that's the word from Mars— the company, not the planet. You know what they say: chocolate lovers are from Mars. Nobody knows where people who don't love chocolate are from.

Also speaking out about the crisis is a company called Barry Callebaut which, I was interested to learn, is one of the world's largest chocolate manufacturers. How did I not know that? I've spent a lifetime studying chocolate, or rather eating it.

One Christmas one of my brothers gave me a year's supply of chocolate—twelve Swiss chocolate bars the size of concrete blocks, one for each month of the year. It was a wonderful gift but I misunderstood. I thought they were for the twelve days of Christmas.

Early in our marriage, my husband bought me a box of Andes Mints, my favorite chocolate-covered mints, for Valentine's Day. On February 15 he asked if he could have one. No, he could not but not because I wasn't willing to share—though I wasn't willing to share.

He couldn't have one because there were none left. He was stunned so I told him I'd been concerned about the freshness date. But he and I both know no chocolate I've ever come in contact with has been in danger of passing its freshness date.

Every year I have to wait until October 30 to buy my Halloween candy. That way there might still be some left by Halloween. But then again, there might not be.

You can see why someone like me would find the news about a chocolate shortage so disturbing.

Apparently it boils down to supply and demand. On the supply side, dry weather, climate change, a tiny moth and a nasty fungal disease are wreaking havoc on the cocoa crop. Let me just say that "tiny moth" and "nasty fungal disease" are a couple of things I don't like hearing in the same sentence as one of my favorite foods—even one of my least favorite foods.

Apparently cocoa farming has become so difficult that many farmers have shifted to more profitable crops like rubber. But who wants to eat that—even with nougat?

On the demand side there's me. And you. The average American consumes around twelve pounds of chocolate every year. I don't take the time to weigh mine before I eat it but I'm pretty sure I get my twelve pounds annually, and quite possibly some of yours as well.

All told, Americans consume around twenty percent of the world's chocolate. Europeans eat about fifty percent of it. That doesn't leave much for anyone else. And that's one reason demand is up. Other countries are catching on. I wonder what took them so long.

Some experts believe the recently discovered health benefits of chocolate may also be driving demand. And there is some evidence suggesting chocolate is good for us. I know that's why I ate my last Snickers bar…for my health.

If you're a chocoholic like I am, you know that dark chocolate has always been considered the more healthful member of the chocolate family. And I do like dark chocolate; I just like it better with milk in it. And sugar.

That's why one study I read about was especially welcome news for me. It supposedly found that any variety of chocolate, not just dark, is associated with reduced risk of cardiovascular disease and stroke. Healthy heart, big butt. I think it's worth it.

Still I'm skeptical. Whenever I read another story about chocolate's health benefits, my first question is who paid for the study? Ghirardelli, Hershey's, Mars? I'm cynical by nature, plus I want to write and thank them.

But if chocolate really is good for us, you can see how it could drive up demand. It's different from a lot of other health foods. You never hear of anyone overdoing it on flax seed. No one eats so many skinless chicken breasts that they can no longer waddle. I'm fond of arugula, but I don't polish off the entire bag every time I have one in the house. But there is no such thing as a bag of chocolates in my house, though there may be some empty bags that once held chocolate.

Still I believe there's a bigger threat on the demand side, and that's the growing enthusiasm for putting chocolate in, on and around everything. Chocolate milk, chocolate covered strawberries and chocolate cereal have all been around awhile. Now we can add chocolate-covered bacon for a complete breakfast.

Chocolate wasters dunk pickles, onions, beef jerky, even roses and wine bottles in chocolate. In other words, they take two things I like and turn them into one thing I don't like at all.

They also dip a few things in chocolate that I never liked to begin with, insects for example. I know many bugs are edible and even nutritious. But so is broccoli and you wouldn't put chocolate on that, would you? Oh wait. That's been done.

But why? What is it about chocolate that makes it so easy to waste? Would you put bubble gum in your chicken noodle soup or grape jelly on your pepperoni pizza? Would you put ants in your ice cream? Not unless you were hell-bent on wasting them all and giving the ants a bad case of hypothermia.

Does anyone in their right mind really think

eating an onion—or a cockroach—with chocolate on it is a good idea? Or are they just trying to shock and disgust us, in which case they could just sneak up behind us and blow their nose really loudly.

I don't know what can be done about the chocolate supply, but on the demand side I have an idea. Stop wasting it! Putting chocolate on pickles and salami is like papering your walls with hundred dollar bills. Or gold-plating cardboard. It's wasteful and not that good anyway. If you have chocolate to waste, give it to me. I'll treat it like the precious commodity it is. Then I'll eat it.

Other books by Dorothy Rosby include:

*I Used to Think I Was Not That Bad and
Then I Got to Know Me Better*
The book for people who read self-improvement
books but never get any better. Also for the
people who sincerely wish they would.

*I Didn't Know You Could Make Birthday
Cake from Scratch; Parenting Blunders
from Cradle to Empty Nest*
The little book of big parenting boo-boos.

*To invite Dorothy to your book
club or other event:*
Dorothy Rosby
605-391-0028
drosby@rushmore.com

To follow Dorothy:
www.dorothyrosby.com
Twitter @dorothyrosby
facebook.com/rosbydorothy